how to start a home-based

Mobile App Developer Business

Chad Brooks

Guilford, Connecticut

Interior spot art licensed by Shutterstock.com

Editorial Director: Cynthia Hughes Cullen
Editor: Meredith Dias
Project Editor: Lauren Brancato
Text Design: Sheryl P. Kober
Layout Artist: Nancy Freeborn

ISBN 978-0-7627-8809-5
ISSN 2332-0826
Printed in the United States of America

10 9 8 7 6 5 4 3 2

Contents

Acknowledgments

Many thanks to all who helped make this book possible. First and foremost are all the wonderful and talented developers, lawyers, social media experts, and business coaches who provided their brilliant insight into the app industry. I would like to specifically thank developers Bryce Avery, Manne Darby, Kevin and Diane Hamilton, Peter Kruger, Alex Genadinik, Caroline Fielding, Tim Lee, Josh Weiss, Andrew Wilcox, Brandon Medenwald, and Benny Hsu; attorney Jason Killips; social media expert Tim Tagaris; and business coaches Mike O'Neal and Jeff Hellenbrand. Together, they spent dozens of hours explaining what it really takes to run a successful home-based app development business. It is because of them that the book holds so much information and advice.

I also offer my sincere appreciation to Tracee Williams, Meredith Dias, and Cynthia Hughes from Globe Pequot Press for taking the chance on me as a first-time author, and working with me throughout the process to make this book, and my dreams of becoming a published author, a reality.

I am also indebted to BusinessNewsDaily editor Jeanette Mulvey. In addition to helping me further my writing career over the past several years, it was her foresight that led me to write about mobile apps to begin with. Without her, I never would have had the chance to fulfill this aspiration.

I would be remiss if I didn't send a special thanks to my parents, Barry and Diane Brooks. From the moment I wanted to be a writer at a young age, they provided me with the support, guidance, and love to make it happen.

Finally, and most importantly, I send my undying gratitude to my wife and daughter, Erin and Mallory Brooks, who give me the encouragement and inspiration each day to be a better writer and a better person. Throughout the process of writing the book, my wife gave me the motivation to keep going. She was a sounding board when I needed advice and an editor when I needed an extra set of eyes. Without her, this book—or the happy life I live—wouldn't be imaginable.

Introduction

You buy them, you use them incessantly, and now you have ideas for your own, so why shouldn't you be cashing in on the mobile app frenzy? With the explosion of smartphones and tablets, mobile apps are being downloaded at a staggering rate—more than thirty million a day. The sheer variety of potential apps—from calculators and games to fitness trackers and grocery lists—is endless, driving both their global popularity and users' desire to get in on a chunk of the action.

The growth of the app marketplace has actually been fueled by everyday consumers, like you, who have turned their idea for the next great app into an at-home development business for relatively low costs. If you're ready to take that idea that's been floating around in your head for the app you think can be the next big thing, this book's for you.

How to Start a Home-based Mobile App Developer Business will serve as a step-by-step guide for app users hoping to cash in on the booming industry, whether they're looking for a full-time business or a part-time operation that can be run on the side.

For those aspiring to build a big company that develops numerous apps, this book will be a road map, allowing you to hear from experts who've created their own success. For those eyeing a smaller operation focused on just a few apps—or those hesitant to get started—the book will provide tips and tricks for getting into the business, with testimonials from those in the trenches who can offer guidance for making it work. Regardless of the route you wish to choose, *How to Start a Home-based Mobile App Developer Business* will let you hear straight from at-home developers who have done it and know exactly what pitfalls to look out for.

While many at-home app developers would rather spend their days focused on the apps and developing the next great idea, it is critical to remember that building an app isn't just about the app itself. Big or small, the principles of running a successful business are the same; they depend on much more than just a good idea. Behind every successful app is a well-run, well-thought-out business, led by those who are prepared for the hard work it will take and the ups and downs that will certainly come their way.

The goal of this book is to leave no stone unturned, giving potential developers everything they need to transform an initial idea into a moneymaking business in an app-hungry society. We'll start at the very beginning: determining if you're even ready and able to run a home-based business of any sort. We will get you asking yourself some tough questions, like "Am I disciplined enough to work from home?" and "Do I have or can I obtain the necessary funds to start a business and keep it running?" If you think you're ready for a home-based business, we will then explore why you think specifically becoming an app developer is the right move for you. Liking and using apps aren't good enough reasons to build a business around them. You need to have the creativity and originality to develop new apps, the discipline and fortitude to run a home-based business, and the mental toughness to handle the highs and lows of being an entrepreneur.

If you think you have that great idea, you might be tempted to start building it, but there are a number of steps that must be taken before the app is anywhere close to the development phase. It is important to remember that this will be about more than just a fun new app that mobile phone and tablet users can play with or use to make their lives simpler. While the apps will be the stars, they will also be the center-piece of a business that needs to be properly formed and run.

This book will guide you through some of those not-so-fun and confusing tasks, like writing a business plan—the core of any successful venture. This isn't just a matter of jotting down a couple of paragraphs stating what kind of business it will be. This is an-depth strategy that not only helps entrepreneurs get their new home-based business up and running, but also provides them with a path to success. Properly preparing any business for both its launch and eventual growth is necessary for every successful business. The only place businesses run themselves is into the ground.

A key component to launching any business is making sure it will be financially viable. In this book, financial planners will guide you through the processes of deciding how much money you are willing to invest in the company and determining where those funds will come from, such as savings or loans from friends, family, or a bank. As an entrepreneur and business owner, it is up to you to spend the necessary time thinking through the development and financial aspects of the business before you are ready to unveil it. Putting in the hours during the planning and organizational stages will only pay off in the long run.

Once you have cemented a strong foundation for the "business" side of the app developer business, you will be able to more freely and easily focus on the "app" side of things. As a developer, there are three key stages to building and selling a profitable app. While you may think your idea is a good one, and some friends and family might have told you how ingenious it is, you still must do a tremendous amount of research to make sure your potential app will thrive in the current marketplace. You will need to investigate current trends, and ensure that the app is not only something that people would use, but something they would pay for as well.

With the research complete, the next step is finally turning that idea into an actual app that can bring financial success. This book will help you determine if you have the right skill sets to build the app on your own, or if you will need to hire an outside developer with coding experience to bring it to life. Both sides have pros and cons, so it is important to understand what each route entails. Once the app has been built—whether it's by you, a high-priced development firm, or a more inexpensive free-lancer—and tested to make sure it is running as intended, it's time to hit the market.

But this book doesn't end with the development stage. It will walk you through the process of getting your app into the hands of smartphone and tablet users by calculating the app's appropriate cost and determining the marketplaces—Apple, Android, or both—in which it will have the most success. Once the app hits Apple's App Store or one of the several Android app marketplaces, you might think you can just sit back and wait for the money to start rolling in. With that approach, though, you'll be waiting quite a while. Finishing the app is only half the journey.

Apps won't sell themselves, so the book will also guide users through the vital marketing stage. Beyond having an initial idea that interests consumers, marketing might be the most important task in running an at-home business. From figuring out how to position the app inside each marketplace to promoting it online, experts who have gone through this important part of the process will give you firsthand tips on how to get your app noticed by as many smartphone and tablet users as possible. The marketing of an app, both after it launches and throughout its life, can easily mean the difference between an app that never gains traction and never makes money and one that has consumers buzzing and money rolling into your pockets.

The question at that point becomes "Do I want to do it again?" This book will help you find that answer and best determine whether you want to keep building a well-run, productive business that features myriad apps, or if you're content being a one-hit wonder who is ready for something different.

How to Start a Home-based Mobile App Developer Business is a necessary read for anyone ready to take the leap but unsure of how to jump. Whether you have a strong business background with no app experience, are an experienced coder with no financial acumen, or neither, I—with help from the experts in the pages to follow—will fill in the gaps with exactly the things you need to know to run a productive, successful, and profitable home-based app developer business.

So You Want to Start a Home-based App Developer Business

If you think having an idea for an app that you personally find to be brilliant is reason enough to start a business, it might be time to think again. Running a business, whether it be as your sole focus or just something you're planning to operate on the side, is a colossal commitment and demands a lot of thought and attention before getting started. From whether you have the time to commit and the drive to succeed to whether you have the finances available to survive, there are major factors that you need to consider before you can even begin to start building your business.

Time

Starting a new business is a tremendous time commitment. A business is not a hobby that you can tend to whenever it's convenient for you. Rather, it requires a significant commitment to doing whatever it takes to succeed. Owning your business is substantially different from working for someone else. While you might have been committed to giving your employer your best efforts, you never had skin in the game. You didn't go to sleep at night worried about whether the company would survive or if the right decisions were being made.

This is not a nine-to-five proposition where you go home at the end of the day and have some carefree nights and weekends, like it can be when working for an employer. When you are the company's founder, boss, and employee all in one, there is no punching the clock and heading home at night. There are eighteen-hour days, weekends filled with work, and, oftentimes in the beginning, not a lot to show for it. If you plan to do this full-time, your life will be consumed by this venture. You will think about it all day and all night—while in the shower, during breakfast and story time with the kids, and while tossing and turning in bed. If this will be a part-time venture, you need to be prepared to give up that time you have to relax each night and on the weekends. Because you're still going to have a full-time job, you need to give each venture the proper respect and attention it deserves. Starting your own business doesn't mean you have the right to slack off with your current employer.

Fielding (see below) underscores just how time-consuming and demanding running a part-time business can be while working full-time. Being able to succeed at both requires the type of drive and focus that Fielding and many other success stories in this field have.

Space

If you are going to work from home, you need to determine where in the house that's going to be. While laptops and tablets make it easier than ever to work from anywhere, that doesn't mean running a home business should be done in front of the television on the living room couch. Your home is filled with distractions. The

Expert's View: Time Management
Caroline Fielding

Caroline Fielding is a part-time app developer who knows this scenario all too well. For the last two years, Fielding, a single mother of two teenage boys, has juggled her newly formed app business with her full-time paralegal position. In 2012 she launched her first mobile app, Bus Rage, a driving game designed to be simultaneously fun and therapeutic.

Because Fielding's app development company, Dryven, Inc., is a one-woman show, the last twenty-four months have been filled with sleepless nights and a lot of questions from her family, friends, and paralegal coworkers about why she has no time for a social life. Instead of hanging out with friends and going out to dinner, Fielding spends her nights tweeting and blogging about Bus Rage.

"I am laser-focused on success, so that's what drives me," Fielding says. "But family and friends sometimes get a little mad because I want to stay in on Saturday nights, posting things on my blog. This is more important to me now at this point in my life. I just stay focused, and, hopefully, in five to ten years, this will all pay off and then I will have time to play."

television, refrigerator, laundry, etc., provide all-too-easy excuses for at-home workers to shirk their responsibilities. You need to set aside space as far away from those distractions as possible so that you can focus on your task at hand, whether that means turning a spare bedroom into an office or getting rid of the man cave in favor of a new "work cave."

It doesn't have to be big or well decorated—just free of distractions. Because you will be developing apps, nearly all of your work, from the research and development to financial record-keeping and marketing, will be done online and via the computer—which means all you really need space for is a desk and chair. As long as the room has Internet and phone access and is free of tempting interruptions, the space will work.

Spending time at a place outside the home also keeps home-based business owners from feeling too isolated. Running a home-based business on your own can be a lonely venture. Especially in a business where nearly all of your work is done online, you can go numerous days without seeing or even talking to anyone. If you are a

Expert's View: Finding a Workspace

Joshua Weiss

Running a home-based business does not mean you have to be chained down to your home at all times. Many home-based business owners prefer working from spaces outside the home, such as coffee shops and libraries, like app developer Joshua Weiss.

After launching his app development company, TeliApp Corporation, in 2010, Weiss spent the first year working solely from home. Fed up with the distractions at home but not wanting to waste money renting office space, Weiss decided instead to spend his days working from places that offered the main amenity needed—public Wi-Fi. From ringing home phones to kids who are constantly in need of something, Weiss says the interruptions became too much of a focus-killer.

"I highly recommend that people who work from home don't. You can still be a guy that works from home, just not physically in the house," Weiss says. "Go to Starbucks, go to Panera Bread—unless you are able to focus and not be distracted even by the simplest things. There is just every excuse in the book. Those are the complications of working from home."

social butterfly, working from home could prove tough to get used to, especially if your home business is your full-time job.

Money

While starting a home-based app development business is not an expensive proposition, you will need some money to get started. Registering as a developer, hiring outside coders if necessary, and marketing all take funds. Before you get rolling you need to make sure you have the necessary finances available. The last thing you want to do is get started only to realize you don't have enough money to finish. You also don't want to start a new business by putting the rest of your finances in jeopardy. If you don't have the funds saved up already, you might want to consider spending six to twelve months saving a start-up pool of cash before diving into things.

Not having the start-up money is not a deal-breaker, however. There are numerous options for small business financing that can help you get on your feet. The first place many entrepreneurs turn to for help is often family and friends. Those who choose this option need to be prepared for the potential consequences. If things go south and for some reason you aren't able to repay the loan, you are putting that personal relationship in jeopardy. You need to weigh the pros of finding someone to give you the money you need against the cons of losing a good friend over cash.

Other financing options include loans from the Small Business Administration (SBA). The SBA offers several types of financing options, including the 7(a) loan program, which offers loans of up to $5 million, and the microloan program, which provides small businesses with loans of up to $50,000. Other choices, each with their own benefits and drawbacks that need to be carefully weighed, include using credit cards, taking out a home equity loan, getting a microfinance loan through an online site such as Kickstarter (a website that lets people try and raise money for a variety of reasons, including starting a business), or finding an angel investor who is willing to put up the capital to kick things off.

Any option you choose needs to come with the understanding that, more than likely, it will take some time before the business starts becoming profitable. This means that if the terms of your loan require you to pay it back relatively quickly, you need to have a plan in place for how you are going to come up with that money. Before taking any money from anyone, you need to carefully establish a realistic strategy for paying it back. Borrowers who take money without a thoughtful payback plan could find themselves and their business fighting their way out of debt for years to come.

Home-based Business Quiz

1. A new home-based business is started how often?

   A: Every 2 days

   B: Every 13 hours

   C: Every 12 seconds

2. How many home-based businesses are there in the United States?

   A: 756,000

   B: 38 million

   C: 234 million

3. What percentage of home-based businesses succeed within three years?

   A: 45 percent

   B: 70 percent

   C: 32 percent

4. What percentage of home-based businesses can be started for less than $5,000?

   A: 44 percent

   B: 75 percent

   C: 17 percent

5. Home-based businesses generate how much combined revenue per year?

   A: $28 million

   B: $176 million

   C: $427 million

—Data courtesy of www.businessforhome.org/2012/07/
home-based-business-in-america

Answer Key: C; B; B; A; C

Motivation

New York City–based developer Alex Genadinik has been working on his series of business start-up–related apps full-time for the past two years, from home. He has learned that entrepreneurs who are motivated to succeed have no trouble overcoming the numerous distractions that come with working from home.

"If they can't focus because the TV is there, or because of entertainment or not having a boss, then that is an intrinsic, internal problem," Genadinik says. "They need to be so motivated that the business is the only thing they can think about. If they aren't motivated naturally, then they need to rethink what they are doing, because this thing will take all of their effort and then some."

He believes that too many people who work from home say that when they are in their house, it is too hard to get motivated. When that's the case, Genadinik says, the home-based business owners are setting themselves up to fail.

Personality

Another major question many eager entrepreneurs fail to ask themselves is whether they are truly the type of people who would be good at running their own businesses. Many people feel much more comfortable working for someone else. They prefer not having to make tough decisions and not having to be a leader, and there's nothing wrong with that—except that it makes for a poor entrepreneur. Entrepreneurs are leaders, decision-makers, self-motivated, and always willing to take on the tough tasks and step up to face the consequences if necessary. They have a willingness to fail if that's what it takes to come out on top in the end, and a competitive spirit that few can rival.

When times get tough, as they most certainly will, there is no one else to turn to for help. The buck starts and stops with you, and that challenge is something all would-be business owners need to be prepared for.

Having you answer these tough questions and look deep inside yourself to see if you have what it takes isn't a way of scaring you off. Rather, it's a reminder that home-based businesses are serious ventures that take a lot of hard work, time, and commitment. Yes, there are a number of benefits that come from running your own business, such as setting your own hours and answering to no one, but the drawbacks can be severe and financially debilitating if not addressed before getting started.

Why Apps?

If you decide after careful deliberation that a home-based business is for you, the next question that you must ask yourself is why you want to start an app development business specifically.

Liking and using apps isn't reason enough to get started in this business. A lot of people like watching television, but that doesn't mean they should jump into the electronics business to start making and selling them. The good news is that, unlike the television industry, which is dominated by a select few, the app industry is open to large and small developers alike.

Controlled Creativity

Getting started in the mobile app industry takes a type of practical creativity that not everyone has. This means that you must be able to come up with unique and innovative ideas—and they must be ideas that can actually be implemented. Simply having an imaginative and creative vision is wonderful, but it will only take you part of the

Knowing the Industry

If you are going to get into the mobile app industry, you should know what it is all about. Here are a few quick statistics courtesy of app analytics firm Flurry and mobile consulting firm mobiThinking to help you get a better feel for the industry you are jumping into:

- There are more than 1 billion app users worldwide.
- Between 56 and 82 billion apps are projected to be downloaded in 2013.
- The average mobile user spends more than two hours a day using apps.
- App users open on average eight different apps per day.
- App owners spend 79 percent of their time using either games or social networking apps.
- The most downloaded apps are games.
- Mobile users can buy apps from more than seventy different app stores.

way in this field. You need to be able to apply those creative ideas to the mobile platform. So, while an idea for an app that does your laundry for you would be amazing, it's not practical. If you are the type of person who has a hard time scaling down and reeling in ideas, this probably isn't the best industry for you.

Possibly most important, mobile app developers cannot be driven by money. Yes, the end goal of everyone in this profession is to hit it big with the next Angry Birds, but it is critical to be realistic about those chances. Recent research has shown that the majority of developers earn less than $40,000 a year off their apps. As with most businesses, the chances of jumping in and hitting it big right off the bat are slim. There is nothing wrong with dreaming big—it's what keeps every entrepreneur moving forward each day—but you must understand that you won't get there overnight, and it certainly won't happen if you're not willing to give this venture all you've got.

You need to want to do this. You need to have a passion and initiative to both drive the app through the difficult and sometimes frustrating development process, as well as spend the necessary time building a business and brand that will eventually, potentially, be about more than just one app. The mobile app industry is here to stay. The question is, are you ready, capable, and committed to becoming part of it?

Chapter Recap

Here is a recap of the questions you need to be asking yourself about your abilities, your work ethic, and your ability to run a successful home-based app developer business.

1. Whether it's full-time or part-time, can I commit enough time and energy to running a home-based business?

Regardless of whether this will be a full-time job or something you do while working another job, running an app development business takes a significant time commitment. If you don't want to commit the time and energy, don't bother getting started.

2. Do I have appropriate space inside my home to run a home-based business?

While it provides exceptional flexibility, working out of the home also comes with numerous distractions. Make sure you have the distraction-free space you will need to efficiently operate a home-based business.

3. Can I handle the isolation that comes with working from home?

When you work from home, there are no coworkers to chat up or bosses to run things by. With most of their critical work being done on a computer, app developers need to be prepared for many days when they don't see another soul during working hours.

4. Do I have the money needed to launch a home-based app developer business?

While it doesn't necessarily take a significant amount of start-up cash, it does take some. If you don't have the money, there are a number of places entrepreneurs can turn to for funding, including more casual sources like family and friends, and more formal options like home equity or SBA loans.

5. Do I have the personality type of a winning entrepreneur?

Entrepreneurs are a special breed. They are fearless and relentless and willing to do everything possible to achieve their goals. If you don't have that drive, running an app development venture might not be for you.

6. Am I comfortable making all the tough choices?

When you run your own business, the buck starts and stops with you. If you can't handle the pressure of making every decision, both easy and difficult, running a business is going to be a difficult proposition for you.

7. Am I creative enough to constantly be developing new consumer-desired apps?

A lot of app developers have one good idea and are unable to come up with anything desirable after that. To be a prosperous developer, you need to constantly be coming up with new app ideas. They won't all be successful, and many won't even make it to the development phase, but without new ideas, your company won't take you very far.

8. Can my creativity be reined in and applied in the mobile app setting?

While you need to be creative, you also need to think of ideas that can easily be translated into an app. You only waste time and energy by trying to think of ideas that are so grandiose and outrageous that they could never really work as a mobile app.

9. Am I doing this just because I want to get rich?

Becoming an at-home app developer is not a quick ticket to becoming a millionaire. While there's always a chance you will hit it big right off the bat, it's just not something you should expect or depend on. If you want a business that will take you into another tax bracket, app development might not be a good fit for you.

10. Now that I know what it takes to be successful, do I still want to become a home-based app developer?

If your answer is no, then you should consider stopping this process before investing any more time or money. If you have the time, space, money, and drive to become a successful entrepreneur, it is time to move on to the next chapter, to start laying out how your business will operate in both the short and long term.

02

Envision Your Business

Now that you know more about being a home-based entrepreneur and the mobile app industry and are eager to move forward, the next step is to put significant thought into how you're going to run your business. It doesn't matter if you want to keep this venture simple and small or become the next major app conglomerate. A detailed and comprehensive plan is well advised regardless. With research showing anywhere from 25 to 40 percent of businesses failing in the first year, it is important to lay out a plan so you don't end up as just another statistic. This is the time to ponder both large- and small-scale aspects of your new business.

Part Time or Full Time?

The first issue you need to address is whether this is going to be an on-the-side business or one you're devoted to full time. The key here is that it doesn't necessarily have to be one or the other. You can have plans to start off small, with expectations to grow in the future. Any direction you choose is perfectly fine—you just need to be prepared for what comes with each option. A number of successful independent app developers recommend starting off slowly and expanding as you learn more about the industry and are able to become more financially viable.

If you aren't financially able to work on your app development full time, you need to develop a plan for how your time will be divided and how you are going to make it work. Saying "I will just work on it during my free time" is not a good-enough answer. You need to set actual work hours and commit to those times. For example, set a schedule for which you spend three hours working on app development on Tuesdays, Wednesdays, and Thursdays, and then spend another six to eight hours working on Saturdays and Sundays. While this will

Expert's View: How Much Time Should I Devote to My Start-Up?

Kevin and Diane Hamilton

The husband-and-wife app development team of Kevin and Diane Hamilton says they started off small, developing apps and making what they termed "hobby money"—low five figures—and, over a number of years, slowly transitioned into doing it full-time. Since releasing their first app for the Mac in 2005—Home Inventory—the couple has founded Binary Formations, which specializes in applications for the Mac as well as for the iPhone, iPad, and iPod Touch. The Hamiltons have now developed five apps, with more on the way. However, before they were able to take app development from a part-time venture to a full-time career, they laid out a careful plan designed to ensure that they could continue supporting their family with their app development earnings.

"Finances were very important. We didn't jump ship completely until we were confident we could live on a certain amount of money coming in. We had a number of steps we took. We didn't just say, 'Okay, we are going to do this on this day,' " Diane Hamilton says.

Among the steps the couple took before diving into full-time app development was a more subtle move to working part-time for their employers and part-time on the app development business. During those eighteen months, the Hamiltons watched their income and expenses closely to ensure that app development was profitable enough for them to make a living.

"We did that so we could go through a year living on the revenue that was coming in from the app, with my part-time salary as the backup," Diane Hamilton says. "We averaged out the revenue that was coming in for the year and made sure we could live on that before I made plans to move over full-time."

Once they saw that they could make it work, Diane quit her job, and the couple has been working full-time for Binary Formations ever since. While plenty of app developers have hit it big while still working for another employer, Kevin Hamilton believes he wouldn't have found success if he hadn't quit his job to work on Binary Formations full-time.

"I do think it is very difficult to have a level of success in something like this without giving it your full attention," Kevin Hamilton says. "I don't think it would have happened if I hadn't quit my job. It needed that level of commitment."

eat up much of your free time, it is really the only way to keep yourself on track. Having enough discipline to stick to your schedule will be half the battle. If you can do it, your path to success will be much shorter.

Type of Apps

Once you have determined how much time you can commit to this venture, you need to start pinning down the types of apps you are going to build. The possibilities are endless. Currently, the Apple App Store and Google Play—the largest Android app marketplace—each has more than twenty different categories of apps. Categories include games, books, entertainment, finances, lifestyle, productivity, social networking, and shopping. While some developers enjoy creating apps that are all over the board, many find success focusing on just one area.

This is a time to get a general feel for the type of apps you want to develop as opposed to spending a lot of time considering a single app idea. Because you will be doing a lot of research once you have chosen your genre, you want to spend this time considering just the type of apps you want to work on. Don't get hung up on details during this stage. Try to focus on the big picture, such as "I want to build games," or "I'd prefer to focus on photo apps." There will be plenty of time to explore your individual apps further. Use this time to think more abstractly about bigger-picture issues, such as what type of apps are potentially going to bring in the most money, or which apps will bring you the most enjoyment during the development stage.

Developer Joshua Weiss says that regardless of the category you choose, you want to make sure the apps you build will target the largest possible audience. The most profitable apps, of course, are those that appeal to the most people.

"There are a lot of apps out there that are great, but they only cater to a small niche audience," Weiss says. "When you cater to a tiny percentage of people, you severely limit the amount of revenue you can generate and the audience you can attain. You want something that's good for most of the people, most of the time."

He cites the wildly popular Angry Birds from Rovio Entertainment as a perfect example of one such app, this one a game that has been a hit with a wide variety of consumers. "Think about Angry Birds, a truly successful app," Weiss says. "It's just a game anyone can play. I play it, and my four-year-old plays it, too."

Besides targeting a large audience, many developers create apps that try to solve some sort of problem—big or small, important or trivial—to generate consumer interest. While some apps are obvious about the problems they solve, such as bill organizers or grocery lists, others are more subtle but still fill a need for consumers.

Another factor to consider when deciding what type of apps to create is whether it is something you will use and enjoy. Kevin Hamilton believes the key for first-time app developers, because they will be devoting so much time and energy to the venture, is to work on something that truly captivates them.

"We aren't interested in building anything that we aren't going to use or like ourselves," Hamilton says. "If it's something that you are interested in, then you'll understand the problem much better. At least you can see how it will solve things for you."

Once you have a better feel for the type of apps you are going to develop, it is time to plan out exactly who is going to do the building.

Who Is Coding the App?

When laying out your business, you want to weigh the pros and cons of trying to build and program the app on your own. For those who have mobile app building experience, programming it on your own will save you a considerable amount of money. It will give you the freedom to build the app exactly the way you envision it,

Expert's View: The Perfect App Idea

Caroline Fielding

Caroline Fielding came up with the idea for her Bus Rage game—which lets users simulate driving a bus back and forth over people who have wronged them—while driving in her car after a particularly long day. She was suddenly cut off by another driver, nearly causing a major accident. It was then, in her moment of internal rage, that Fielding came up with the app idea.

"I thought, 'You know, I wish I could do something in real life that would not really hurt her, but kind of make it seem that way,' " Fielding says. "I thought, 'I wonder if there's an app for that?' The idea came to life, just like that."

While Fielding's problem isn't a big one, her Bus Rage game is a way to fill the need she has. Regardless of the type of apps you choose to develop, it is important to try and tap into people's needs. Those needs and problems will be the driving force behind a consumer's decision on whether or not to buy your apps.

without having to struggle through the sometimes difficult process of describing your vision to someone else. The key is understanding just how proficient you are in working with Objective-C or Java. People with no previous experience can build apps, but if you plan to make money doing it, it had better work as described and have a polished and professional look. This means you'd better have a good understanding of the programming code, its features, and how they all work.

Brandon Medenwald, cofounder of Simply Made Apps, says that programmers who don't have any experience working with Apple's coding program, Objective-C, shouldn't be scared off from working with the new medium.

"If you have any amount of programming experience in almost anything, coming up to speed [on Objective-C] is not hard," says Medenwald, whose first app, Simple In/ Out, was released in 2011. "The best way to learn is to just grab a couple of tutorials and start playing around. It is going to take time, but if you spend a couple of hours a week, you'll get a long way after a month or two."

While building and coding apps on your own is cheaper than the alternative— hiring an outside developer—it does still come with a price. Actually building the app can be the most painstaking aspect of the entire process. Depending on its complexity, it can take anywhere from six to eighteen months to build an impressive, consumer-worthy app. Even if you are an expert coder, you need to weigh the cost of paying a professional to build the app against the number of hours it will take you to do it on your own. If you plan to work for someone else while this venture gets off the ground, be prepared for many late nights staring at your computer screen.

For those with no coding experience or who don't want to learn how to build mobile apps specifically, there are two options. The first is to use a service that helps you do all of the building without having to know anything about coding. These types of services, such as AppsBuilder and AppMakr, are do-it-yourself platforms that can cost as little as $50 to $100. The drawback is that you are using their templates and designs, which takes a lot of the creativity out of your hands. They also don't have as many feature possibilities as you would if you were coding the app from scratch. However, if you are looking to get something developed and in the app store quickly, this might be your best bet.

The second option is to hire an outside developer who will work directly with you to build, program, and code your app. From individual freelancers in every corner of the world to large conglomerates in the United States, the range and sheer number of developers is immense. These outside developers are charged with taking your vision and turning it into an actual app. You will work closely with them throughout the developmental and testing stages to ensure that the app they build is what you imagined and expected.

Among the development options, this is definitely the most costly of the three. Hiring an outside developer can range anywhere from one thousand to hundreds of thousands of dollars, depending on how robust and sophisticated you want your app to be. If you are going to go this route, you need to start considering how much money you want—and can afford—to spend on each app. Knowing how much you are prepared to spend will make the process of choosing a developer that's right for you significantly easier.

While we will explore in much greater detail the process of finding, hiring, and working with an outside developer in chapter 8, try to determine now if this is the route you are planning to go so that you will have a better idea of the start-up finances necessary to get your first app off the ground.

Once you know who is building your new app, it is time to put some thought into the devices you want them to run on.

Apple vs. Android

The next issue to contemplate is whether or not you plan to build the app for the Apple or Android operating system. Because the two platforms are totally different, using complexly different design environment and tools, you need to think about which platform will not only best suit your needs, but will also help you to bring in the most money.

The biggest technical difference between the two is the programming language each uses. Apple features the Objective-C programming code, while Android employs Java. For those who don't plan to do any coding on their own, programming language won't really have an impact on their decision. Those who do plan to do the coding without any outside help will most likely be inclined to go with the programming language they feel most comfortable using.

Brandon Medenwald's Simply Made Apps has released its mobile app, Simple In/ Out, on both platforms, and he knows the pros and cons of working with each from a technical perspective. Like many others, Medenwald agrees that the Apple platform and tools are much easier to use than those Android offers.

"The biggest difference is what you can accomplish visually in a short period of time," Medenwald says. "The tools that Apple provides for the iOS platform allow you

Quick Look: Apple vs. Android

Apple App Store

- The Apple App Store is the only place to legally buy iOS apps.
- Apple takes a 30 percent cut from every app sold in the Apple App Store.
- As of January 2013, Apple users have downloaded more than 40 billion apps, with nearly 20 billion in 2012 alone.
- There are approximately 775,000 apps in the Apple App Store, 330,000 of which are for iPad.
- Apple has paid developers $7 billion since the store's opening in 2008.
- The Apple App Store offers mobile apps to users in more than 150 different countries.
- The App Store has more than 500 million active accounts.

The Android Marketplace

- Android apps are sold through multiple outlets.
- There are currently nearly 700,000 Android apps in the market.
- The two most popular Android marketplaces are Google Play and the Amazon Appstore.
- Google and Amazon each take a 30 percent cut from every app sold in the Google Play Store or Amazon Appstore.
- As of July 2012, there were 600,000 apps in the Google Play Store.
- As of September 2012, there were just over 50,000 apps in the Amazon Appstore.
- Consumers have downloaded more than 20 billion apps from the Google Play Store since opening in 2009.
- The Amazon Appstore reports "hundreds of millions" of app downloads since opening in 2011.
- The Google Play Store sells to consumers in more than 130 countries.
- The Amazon Appstore sells to consumers in 200 countries.

—Data courtesy of Apple, Android, Google, and Amazon

to, almost by default, build something that looks pretty good. On the Android side, what you build by default looks very spartan. There isn't a lot there."

In the end, however, a number of app developers believe your choice should center around money. You want to put your resources into developing apps for the platform that is going to bring you the most money. To do that, you need to spend some time researching more marketplaces. You want to understand who the users are of each phone, and which ones are going to be most likely to spend money on your app.

A Legal Brief

As you are starting to envision your business, you might be coming to the realization that you might need some legal advice along the way. Because you are going to be putting time, energy, and money into this venture, you want to be positive that all your legal bases are covered.

Detroit, Michigan, attorney Jason Killips, who has specialized in intellectual property and business litigation for the past decade, says he would advise anyone starting his or her own business to consult with a lawyer early on in the process.

"The best reason to do that is because you don't know what you don't know," Killips says.

Depending on the nature of your business, Killips says there could be many inherent risks from which you need to protect yourself. There could be statutes that you are unaware of that require you to do certain things before you can start conducting a business, or there just might be things you need to start thinking about regarding how you set up your business, such as whether or not to become an LLC or use nondisclosure agreements.

"There are certain businesses where things like that are critically important, but if you don't know about them, or just haven't thought of those issues, you don't even know to take that into account when you are setting up how to do business," he says. "Just getting a lay of the land of the business you are thinking of entering into and getting an understanding for the legal risks that other people in your business have, and that you need to start planning for—those are the best reasons to probably talk to a lawyer right away."

From the perspective of someone who has developed and sold apps on both platforms, Medenwald would strongly advise first-time app developers to put their efforts behind building an iOS mobile app.

"I would encourage people to look at that platform first if you are looking to make money," Medenwald says. "Far more people buy things on the iOS platform than the Android. Our iOS market is a lot more vibrant. For every download we get on Android, we probably do thirty on iOS."

While financial factors often push developers to choose just one platform, Medenwald says there could be benefits to operating on both Android and Apple, depending on the type of app you're planning to release. Medenwald's Simple In/Out app is designed as a way for businesses to easily track their employees' status. He says they chose to develop the app for both platforms to ensure that businesses wouldn't be constricted by having to have all their employees using either strictly Apple or Android devices.

"We needed to make sure we were on both. In order to attract a company, which is primarily the people who use our software, we need to have a certain amount of buy-in," Medenwald says. "There needs to be more than one person in the organization that wants to do it. Invariably there will always be someone on one platform or the other. They might be mostly an Apple shop or mostly an Android shop, but there are always a couple of people on the other side, and unless you can get them to buy in as well, you're dead in the water."

Regardless of which platform you choose, you will never be bound only to that decision. If you pick Apple, for example, and see success, you can always go back and develop your app for Android. However, until you know the app is going to be a hit with consumers, it's best to focus on one or the other, unless your app fulfills specific needs for both.

Business Plans

Now that you have the basic framework for your business, you need to spend time putting pen to paper and writing it all out in a business plan. Even though you likely have put a lot of thought already into your new home-based mobile app developer business, it is important to put those thoughts down on paper so you have them as a reference later. Business plans help to define your operation, set goals, and provide you with a clear path toward success. For those seeking funding, they also serve as an important tool to help woo potential investors by showing them what you plan to accomplish, and how.

Those starting out part-time with the business might feel that writing a business plan is a waste of time that only delays the process of actually building and selling the app, but that's not the case. It doesn't matter whether you are spending only a few hours a week working on the project, or every waking second; you still have goals, and a business plan helps to set you on the path toward accomplishing them. Additionally, if you decide to transition from part- to full-time in the future and require an influx of funding, your business plan will show potential investors how serious you've been about this venture from the start. (Remember to provide them with a clear explanation of how you will earn enough money to pay them back.)

Among the items in a well-thought-out business plan are a company description, market research, a marketing plan, and financial projections—both short- and long-term. Among the specific items that the US Small Business Administration (SBA) recommends including in a formal business plan are:

- Executive summary: A quick overview of your business and what's included in the business plan.
- Company description: Details on your business, what the business will entail, and how you will set yourself apart from others in the industry, as well as who your consumers are.
- Market analysis: Details on the mobile app industry and potential competitors.
- Organization and management: Quickly outline who will be working in the company and the role each will play. Most likely it will just be you, so be sure to include all the roles you will be taking on.
- Product line: Use this opportunity to share a bit about the type of apps you plan to sell and how they will appeal to consumers.
- Marketing and sales: Successful apps rely on a solid marketing plan, so spell out how you plan to entice mobile device users into buying your app. (This will be covered in detail in chapters 11 and 12.)
- Funding request: If you are using the business plan to help attract investors, you need to include some specifics in your funding request, including how much money you are requesting, how much you may need in the future, what you intend to do with those funds, and how you intend to pay them back.

- Financial projections: Include prospective financial data, including forecasted income statements, balance sheets, cash flow statements, and capital expenditure budgets.

To help get you started, you can find a variety of business plan templates online, including several offered by the SBA. From there, you can simply start filling in each field. For those of you who need a little help writing their business plan, you can buy special computer software that will guide you through the entire process. While it is still up to you to come up with what to include in the plan, the software—which can range anywhere from $20 to $150—helps you compile it in a professional format.

Business plan software also features a wide range of research tools to help you with your market analysis, and forecasting tools to assist with financial projections. Some of the most highly rated business plan software packages are Business Plan Pro, BizPlan Builder, Ultimate Business Planner, Business PlanMaker Professional, and Plan Write for Business.

For those who want to keep the business plan–writing process close to home, so to speak, there are ironically now mobile apps to help. Similar to the software, they are designed to help you gather your ideas and present them in a clear and professional way. Available for both mobile phones and tablets, the apps can range from free to as much as $10. Business plan apps include Business Plan Creator, Business Plan Pro Premier, Business Plan & Start Startup, Elevatr, and Business Plan Mobile Pro.

What's key to remember about your business plan is that it isn't a document you write, throw in a drawer, and occasionally reference. This is a constantly evolving document that should always be updated. Your business will evolve and grow from your initial vision. As things change, make sure your business plan keeps in step. Even if it is just updating new financial projections, spend time every month ensuring that your plan is updated. You never know when a potential investor may pop up; you need to be ready for them. Having a professional and updated business plan that you can present within moments is a clear sign that you are serious and dedicated to this endeavor.

Chapter Recap

Here is a recap of the items you need to consider when envisioning your home-based mobile app developer business:

1. Is this going to be a full- or part-time venture?

If you plan to commit yourself full time, make sure you have enough money to live off while your company is getting going. If you go part time, make sure you construct a clear schedule of how you will divide your time between your full-time job, app development, and family and social life.

2. What kind of apps are you going to develop?

You don't need specifics right now, just a general of idea of the type of apps—such as those that focus on games, social networking, or photos—you want to develop. This helps to keep you focused during the research stage of the app development process.

3. Who will build your apps?

If you have programming experience, learning the programming language for both Apple and Android is a relatively easy process. Building it yourself will save you money, but it does require a significant amount of work. If you don't have any programming experience, there are thousands of developers, large and small, who are ready, willing, and able to build what you are looking for—all for a cost, of course. While not highly recommended, do-it-yourself services are available for those looking to build an app on the cheap.

4. Will you build for Apple or Android?

Because the two platforms are completely different, most developers tend to choose one over the other at first. Developers I spoke with recommend trying Apple's iOS platform first if your goal is to make money.

Once you have a solid vision for your business, you need to start establishing it formally. Even though it might seem premature to start forming a company around an app or apps whose success is unknown, that's not the case. To make this a business, you need to treat it like one.

This is not a hobby or something you are doing for fun. While you hopefully will enjoy doing this, your main priority as a business owner is to make money. If you don't, this venture is going to be over before you really get started. Your first step toward making this undertaking profitable is to formally separate it from any other hobbies or activities.

Even if you're doing this on the side, you want to take the time to build a professional operation to set yourself up for success and protect yourself legally. To do that, there are a number of financial and legal steps you need to take.

Luckily, this is going to be a small—most likely one-person—company run from the comfort of your home, so there are many pieces to opening a new business, such as finding a location and hiring employees, that you won't need to worry about.

You do, however, need to determine your business's legal structure, register it with the state in which you live, get the proper state licenses, and obtain a tax identification number.

Choosing a Name and Domain Name

But before you do any of that, you need to choose a company name. Remember, this is different from your mobile app name. Hopefully, you are going to develop numerous apps, all of which will fall under your business's umbrella.

Ideally, you want your name to be something that's catchy, short, easy to remember, and has something to do with apps or development. However, the only real requirement is that someone else isn't already using it.

Another factor to consider is whether there is a matching available domain name. A domain name is a website's address, and after you launch your business, you will want to create an online home for it. To be effective, the domain name should really match the business's name. For example, if I want to name my company "Chad'sApps," I need to make sure that the domain address "www.chadsapps.com" is available.

While this might seem trivial at this stage, it won't be in the future. Should your company become large and successful, you don't want to have the added chore of trying to hunt down the domain address you need. You will end up wasting time and money trying to wrangle it away from someone else.

Don't worry about actually building your company website; that doesn't need to happen for a while. The key is simply ensuring that you own the domain address you want, so when the time does come to launch a company website, you can.

Once you have a name picked out that isn't being used, and you've determined that a corresponding domain address is available (see more about this in chapter 11), you can move forward with founding your business legally and financially.

Legal Structure

Once you have picked a name for your business, the next step to formally establishing your business is to choose a legal structure. This is a critical decision because it helps to determine how you pay your taxes and the type of legal protection you and your business may receive.

There are five main types of business legal structures: sole proprietorship, limited liability company (LLC), corporation, S corporation, and partnership. Assuming you are founding and running this business on your own, your main choices are:

- **Sole proprietorship:** This is the easiest option, but it provides the least amount of legal protection. If you are choosing this, no formal action is required because, according to the Small Business Administration, that status automatically comes from your business activities. Your business is not taxed separately. Any income and expenses are reported on the standard IRS 1040 Form. The downside is that, because there is no legal division between you and your business, you could be personally held liable for any legal action brought against you. This means that if someone sues your company, your personal money, home, or other assets could be used to pay for any damages.

- **Limited liability company:** An LLC combines the benefits of a partnership and corporation by giving owners personal liability protection and special tax breaks. The main advantage of this option is the liability protection it provides business owners. Setting up this structure provides a safeguard against being held personally responsible for any debts or lawsuits that your business incurs. In addition, the business isn't required to pay federal taxes. Instead, the business's profits and losses are passed on to you, and you pay personal income taxes on it. This avoids instances of double taxation. The main downside to this approach is that you would be subject to the higher self-employment tax that LLC owners have to pay.

- **S corporation:** Of the three choices, an S corporation can be the most difficult to set up and the most tedious to run. Much like an LLC, S corporations are subject to limited liability if legal action is brought against the company. It also is similar to an LLC in that owners don't face double taxation. Where it differs is in how this business is formally run. With an S corporation, an increased number of operating rules must be adhered to—holding regularly scheduled director and shareholder meetings, taking minutes at those meetings, and constant stock transfer and record maintenance—and there are regulations requiring that the owner be paid a salary, regardless of whether or not the company is making any money.

While not required, this is an area where you would probably benefit from meeting with a business attorney to determine which option makes the most sense for you, from both a financial and legal perspective. In addition to providing advice, attorneys can also help you fill out the required documents needed to formalize your legal structure.

If you don't use an attorney, it is critical that you properly fill out the required documents for each structure. If you decide to move forward as a sole proprietorship, there is nothing more you need to do except actually run your business. Doing so is the only thing that is needed to formalize your business in this structure.

However, if you are setting up as an LLC, there are several steps you are required to follow to make your business official. With an LLC you must file Articles of Organization with the secretary of state's office where you live. These documents spell out some of the basic information about your company, including its name, owners, and address. In addition to filing the Articles of Organization, some states require new LLCs to announce their opening by publishing news of it in the local media, so it is critical to research exactly what your state mandates before moving forward.

To establish your business as an S corporation, the main steps you must take are to fill out and file the Articles of Incorporation form with the secretary of state's office where you live. Similar to the Articles of Organization, this form spells out the basics of the business, including the name, address, purpose, and incorporators.

You must also fill out IRS Form 2553, "Election by a Small Business Corporation." The form, found on the IRS website, is the document on which you elect to pursue S corporation status. The form must be filed by March 15 of the tax year during which you choose to convert to an S corporation. The IRS will then review those documents to determine whether you meet the eligibility requirements for S corporation status, such as being a domestic company, having no more than one hundred shareholders, and issuing only one class of stock.

Once you have taken steps to set up for business from a legal standpoint, you need to move on to separating it financially.

Opening a Bank Account

One of the most important steps to separating your business from your personal assets is opening a company bank account. Keeping track of how much money the business is spending and bringing in can be difficult if the transactions are mixed in with daily expenses, like trips to the gas station or grocery store.

Running a business requires having a precise understanding of your financial status at all times. The best way to do that is by making sure your personal and business finances are completely separate. In the end, the money will all go back to the same place—you. But opening a separate bank account will help you judge more efficiently the successes or troubles the business is having.

Another advantage of having a separate bank account is that, come tax time, it makes the process go more smoothly. Your accountant or tax preparer will be extremely grateful that he or she won't have to look through a year of your expenses and revenue to determine what was business and what was personal.

If you have chosen either an LLC or S corporation as your legal structure, there are a number of tax breaks you will want to take advantage of. The best way to do that is to have a separate bank account.

Additionally, without a separate bank account, you run the risk of not being able to take advantage of the legal protections that an LLC or an S corporation would provide. It would be a shame to set up an LLC structure to protect yourself from a lawsuit only to find out that your personal finances are still at risk because you never opened a separate business bank account. That is a risk not worth taking.

When opening a business checking account, you should visit the bank where you do your personal banking to inquire whether they have any special rates for opening a new account. You don't need any type of high-level savings accounts or investment accounts at this time. All you need is a checking account that can handle deposits and expenses.

Once you have your account set up, you will be using it to collect payments from each of the app stores where your mobile app is being sold. For example, if you decide to develop apps for Apple's iOS platform, you will become an Apple developer. As part of that, you will need to provide your bank account information to Apple, which will deposit your money into that account when your apps eventually start making money.

Expert's View: Bank Accounts

Mike O'Neal

Texas business coach Mike O'Neal has been counseling entrepreneurs and solopreneurs for the last several years. Part of his advice to his students is to always open a separate bank account for the business, regardless of its legal structure.

"You need to go ahead and separate your business from your personal," O'Neal says. "Even from a sole proprietor standpoint, it is all going to come back to the same pot. But if you keep them separate, your chances of running your business as a business are going to be greatly enhanced."

O'Neal, who teaches a three-part course for entrepreneurs on how to set up and run a new business, says opening a separate bank account is extra critical for companies choosing an LLC structure. Without it, he says, business owners run the risk of not being protected in the event of a lawsuit. "If you do not keep your money separate, what happens is that if you get sued, a lawyer for that other side will attempt to pierce that veil and go after your personal assets, particularly if your personal assets outnumber your business assets, which they typically do for a small company."

If you only have a personal banking account, it will be easy for these app store payments to get lost in the mix and become improperly accounted for from a business standpoint.

Depending on your bank and the legal structure you have chosen for your business, you may need to get a business tax ID number, also known as an Employer Identification Number (EIN), from the IRS. Even if you don't have any employees, some banks still require this number to open a business account. To get your EIN, visit the IRS website at www.irs.gov. From there, you have the option of either applying directly online or printing out the forms to apply via fax. If you would prefer to use the phone, you can obtain an EIN immediately by calling the IRS Business and Specialty Tax Line at (800) 829-4933.

Many businesses also open a credit card account. This isn't a decision to be made lightly. I would advise you to seriously consider whether this is necessary, and what kind of impact an additional credit card will have on your finances. If you are disciplined enough to have one, there is no harm in applying for one through your bank. But if you don't have the self-control to only use it for business purposes, you would be better off not going through the hassle.

Money

Now that you have a bank account for your business, you need something to go in it. How much money you'll need to launch your business is a significant variable. It really comes down to how much you want to invest. While this won't necessarily be the case for you, in general, the more money you invest, the more likely you will be to have a successful app.

The biggest expense really is programming. If you are programming and coding the app yourself, your start-up costs are going to be much lower. If, however, you have no programming experience and will need to hire someone to build the app, you will need a much larger sum to get started; how much larger is up to you.

App developers can hire outside programmers for as little as a few hundred dollars to more than a few hundred thousand dollars. The cheaper options involve hiring a freelance coder through an online site like Elance.com or Freelancer.com. These sites will match you up with programmers whose fees typically run less than $5,000.

The more expensive option is to hire a digital agency to build the app. In addition to most likely putting out a more professional product, digital agencies have a whole team of programmers, each with his or her own specialty, working on your app. While you may get a higher-end product, it is going to cost you significantly more to get there.

Digital agencies can charge anywhere from $10,000 to $100,000 to build the app you are looking for. It all comes down to how much money you have saved up and how much of it you are willing to invest in this initial app. You would probably be best served by not holding back. If your first app isn't very good, you may never get a chance to invest in a second one.

While the programmer can be the most expensive cost of opening a home-based app development business, there are other costs involved. The other things you may need to spend money on include:

- Computer equipment: If you're programming the app yourself, you will need some powerful computer equipment. Even if you're not, having an iMac, especially if you are developing for Apple, will be beneficial in the long run.
- Registering as a developer: Before you can start selling your apps, you will need to pay a developer's fee to each of the app stores you plan to be in. Apple charges $99, while Google Play charges just $25. While minimal, these fees are critical: If you don't pay them, you won't be able to sell your apps.
- Marketing: This is another area where you have the option to spend a little or a lot. However, unlike with programming, the value of spending money on marketing isn't as clear-cut. From buying Google AdWords to hiring a public relations firm to build a publicity campaign around your app, there is a wide variety of options, each with its own price tag. Other potential marketing expenses include building and maintaining a website for the app.
- Professional services: If this is your first business, you likely are going to need to hire some experts to help you launch and run it. At the very least, hiring a lawyer to help get your legal structure properly set up and an accountant to help keep track of your books and pay your taxes might very well be your best option.
- Miscellaneous: As with any business, there are going to be a number of odds and ends, such as equipment breakdown or unforeseen expenses from freelancers or digital agencies, that you will want to have some money saved up for.

In the end, opening a home-based app development business depends on how much you want to spend. That flexibility in how much you need to get started is one of the reasons becoming a developer has become so popular.

Odds and Ends

Because you are, for now, running a one-person operation from your home, there are a number of other registration steps to setting up a business that you aren't subject to. Every state is different, however, so you do need to check with your secretary of state's office to ensure that your new company doesn't need any other licenses or permits.

It is important to make sure everything from a structural standpoint is on the up and up with the state so you don't run into problems down the line when you start selling your apps and making money. You don't want to find yourself facing fines or other punishments because you didn't check things out before getting started.

Some of the other tasks you will want to consider when officially establishing your business are:

- Registered agent: Depending on the legal structure you have selected, you may be required to name the company's registered agent. This is a person who has the legal authority to accept legal and tax documents on behalf of the business. A registered agent is required when setting up a business as an LLC or corporation. You, as the company owner, can also serve as the registered agent, though you certainly don't have to do so.
- Insurance: If you plan to do all the programming of the apps yourself, you most likely will be using some heavy-powered and expensive computer equipment. It is vital that you make sure your homeowner's or renter's insurance policy covers all the equipment you are using. If it doesn't, you would be wise to spend some more for a more robust policy to ensure that your equipment is protected from theft or damage.
- Trademark protection: Once you establish a company name and potentially a company logo, you may want to think about protecting them from being used by anyone else. According to the United States Patent and Trademark Office (USPTO), a trademark is a word, phrase, symbol, and/or design that identifies and distinguishes the source of the goods of one party from those of others. To first see if your name can be trademarked and then file for the protection, visit the USPTO website at www.uspto.gov/trademarks/index.jsp.

With these few steps, you have officially formed a business, and can move on to the process of developing your very first mobile app.

Chapter Recap

Even though you haven't programmed a line of code yet and have nothing to sell anyone, you still want to start the process of officially forming your business. This is necessary to help you define this as an actual business rather than simply a hobby.

When setting up your business, there are several key steps you must take:

- Business name: You need to pick a name for your business. The most important requirements when choosing a name are that it is not currently being used and that its corresponding domain name is available for you to use.

- Legal structure: One of the key aspects of forming a business is choosing a legal structure. For your purposes, your choices are between running a sole proprietorship, an LLC, or an S corporation. Each has various legal and tax pros and cons, so it is important to research each to select which one best meets your needs. When choosing a legal structure, it is critical to file the proper paperwork in your state to register your business.

- Bank account: To best divide your business's finances from your personal ones, you need a separate bank account. This helps you to track your business's expenses and revenue to determine profitability, and also helps to ensure that your personal finances are protected from any legal action brought against the business.

- Money: While there isn't a defined amount as to how much it will take to start your business, be assured that you will need some seed money. Your expenses will include registering as a developer, possibly hiring a programmer to build the app, and creating a successful marketing campaign, including building a website.

- Extras: Other factors you want to think about when forming a new business are whether you need a business credit card to help cover some of your expenses; whether you need extra homeowner's or renter's insurance to protect high-powered computer equipment you may be using; and whether you need your company's name and eventual logo legally protected with a trademark.

04 Researching the Marketplace

Before you can move forward with the app development process, you want to pin down exactly what kind of app or apps you plan to develop. While you likely started down this business path because of a great idea, at this point the idea is only great to you.

Before spending thousands of dollars and countless hours developing your app, you must make sure it is something mobile device owners think would bring value or fun to their lives. Even though you are certain your app will be a huge hit, there are a number of things you need to spend time researching before you can start programming.

There are two stages to the process: The first is to determine if your app has appeal and the potential to be profitable. The second is to determine, based on what is working well for other apps, the best design and interface directions. But, before you can focus on what the app should look like, you want to determine if it is something mobile device owners would even be interested in using.

Getting Perspective

The first step is to start asking friends and family what they think of the idea. While you won't always get the honest truth, especially if they don't like it, they are a good place to start. If they say they don't like your app idea or if they don't understand it right off the bat, then it may be dead before you ever get started.

Another test is to see if they understand the app. When describing your idea, try to gauge whether or not they are following along. Does it seem to click right away in their minds, or does it seem like they are struggling to grasp your concept?

If they are having trouble understanding what the app would do or why it would be valuable, you probably need to go in a different direction or start tweaking your idea.

The optimal reaction is an immediate awareness of the app you are describing and its potential benefits. While this isn't going to tell you if your app has a chance to be a hit, it does give a good indication of whether or not your app is a dud.

Don't be afraid to walk away from a bad idea. The worst thing you can do is keep pushing a bad app idea through to completion. Besides the loss of time and money, it delays your chance to start building your business in a positive direction.

If friends and family do seem to catch on to the idea quickly and give some encouraging feedback, it's time to start doing a little more extensive research.

The Competition

Once you think you have an idea worth pursuing, you want to find out if the app already exists—or, if it doesn't, what similar apps might be available already. More than likely, your idea isn't something so unique and revolutionary that it has no competition. The majority of apps have competitors that don't offer exactly the same features and experience but provide something pretty similar. There is nothing wrong with that.

Don't be scared if you see others doing something similar. It can be a good thing. Use these competitors to your advantage by researching what success their app is having. If the app has had some success and you think yours is even better than what is out there, then you can reasonably expect to find similar, if not greater, success.

When you find apps that are similar to your idea, spend time studying them to see what works and what doesn't. Are there certain features you can improve on? Is there a missing piece that you can add that would make it better? If you are going to develop an app that has competitors, it is critical that you make yours stand out from the crowd.

The competition can also tell you a lot about the consumers and what they are after. That's why, in addition to knowing your competitors, you need to figure out which apps are seeing the most success. By looking at the features and functionality of the best-selling competitors, you can get a better picture of what is driving your target audience to spend money on an app. Be sure to take those features into consideration when you start designing something better.

If you don't find any app with a theme similar to what you want to develop, don't start jumping for joy just yet, thinking you are ready to hit it big. Reinventing the wheel can be much harder than it looks. You really need to find out why there isn't any competition. While there is a chance that no one has thought of your idea before, there is just as good a chance that someone has—and already determined that it can't work.

There are several options for researching what's out there. The first is doing some searches within the app stores themselves. Go to each one—Apple, Google, Amazon, etc.—and start plugging in some search terms that are related to your app idea. Even if you don't plan to develop for each of the different operating platforms, it is still important to check out each store to see if something similar to your app already has gone public. Just because it's not on the operating system you are building it for doesn't mean it's not a competitor and that it can't provide valuable information during your research process.

When plugging in search words, use terms that are both broad and specific. Don't leave any stone unturned when searching for a competitor; try as many search terms as you can possibly think of. You want to see as many different results as possible.

There also are several online search engines devoted specifically to mobile apps. One is http://uquery.com, which has a complete index of every app in the Apple App Store. App-review website www.appolicious.com also has extensive listings of both Apple and Android apps.

It is critical that you know what's out there before getting started. The last thing you want is to get your app developed only to realize after the fact that there is already a more established app doing either exactly what yours does, or something better.

App Design and Function

While learning about the competition is one step of the research process, it's not the only part that is going to help you to develop a winning app. Beyond seeing who else is doing what you want to do, you should also use the research stage to study other types of apps. Because you will be designing your app top to bottom from scratch, you want to have a good idea of the design features you think it should have.

The best way to do this is to look at the apps you use on a regular basis. There is a reason you are drawn to these apps, and it is important to really think about why. Study their interface and layout. Are there some you like better than others? Are there styles you feel are more pleasing to the eye or functions that are easier to use?

Study them carefully, and think about what makes the apps successful and consumer-friendly. Remember, someone like you is probably your target audience, so don't look past your innate ability to know what makes an app worth buying.

Every time you use an app and see something you like, write it down. You want detailed notes of things you like about apps so when it comes time to start designing one of your own, you have examples of exactly what you are envisioning.

In addition to the apps you use on a regular basis, you should also be studying what the top-rated apps offer from a design standpoint. Some of these

How I Did It

Peter Kruger, Rock Lobby

Peter Kruger was wrapping up his first year of working toward his MBA when he started developing Rock Lobby, an app designed to power local live music discovery with real-time fan-based reviews. The New York City developer says he was able to put a lot of his schooling to good use, especially during the research stage.

Kruger says he and his partner spent a lot of time researching what other music- and concert-related apps were out there, and what each brought to the table.

"We set up Excel documents where we figured out all of the features of Rock Lobby that we wanted to have in the beginning, and all of the features we wanted to bring in later on," Kruger says. "We started putting competitors [that had those features] in a column and giving each of them scores. We then did some analytics and created a map to see how much these competitors crossed over, how much of a threat they were to us, and how they all interacted together."

Kruger says that this provided a good picture of the marketplace and how they could fit in and prosper.

"You figure out your place in the market to see if it's viable and see if there is potential," he says. "That was the competitive stuff. Then you can look at the landscape to see where people are investing, and decide: Is this going to be hot, or is this going to be crowded?"

Kruger thinks starting an app development business was the perfect complement to his MBA studies.

"I think it should probably be a normal part of business school," Kruger says. "It is the missing lab component. You are working on something real, so the lessons in the class have a lot more resonance."

highly rated apps have been at the top for a long time. They work from a design, functionality, and entertainment perspective, so there is a lot you can learn from them.

You want to pick and choose the best parts of each app when designing your own. Maybe one app has a database you like best, while another has a design and style you think is the most appealing. Though it might not all be possible by the time you get to the programming stage, this is the time to dream big and come up with the perfect app.

With that in mind, you also want to look at apps that you don't particularly like, and ask yourself why. What about it makes it unappealing? Is it too slow? Does it have a difficult-to-use interface, or a color scheme that is off-putting? There are thousands of dud apps in each app store, and it is important to consider what made them falter so you don't end up with a similar fate.

Add these details to your design notes. Be sure to specify the things that don't work so you aren't wasting time during the programming phase, building features that don't work well or using graphics and design styles that end up being hard to read.

The better you can pinpoint exactly what works and what doesn't, the more efficient the rest of your app's development is going to be. The efficiency will help save you time and money, and it will help you to produce a better end product.

App Pricing Strategies

The final thing you need to study during the research stage is how other apps are making money. As we have discussed, this is a business, and your end goal is not just developing a consumer-friendly app, but also developing an app that makes you money. There are several different ways to make money off a mobile app, so it is important to figure out which one will be best for you. Pick the wrong strategy and it won't matter how your app looks or works, because it won't be making you any money when it's finished.

The first places to start researching monetization options are the same places you've been doing all your other research: your app's competitors, the apps you like best, and the top-rated apps. These apps are filled with information that can help make creating your pricing strategy—one of the toughest parts of the development process—a lot easier. Each time you study one of these apps, take a look at how the developer is turning a profit off it, if at all. There are three different monetization strategies that mobile app developers use: paid downloads, in-app purchasing, and in-app advertising.

Each strategy has its pluses and minuses, which we will explore in chapter 10, so you to want to determine which ones are or aren't working for your competitors. For example, if all the competitors are offering free apps with in-app advertising, it's telling you there isn't much of a market for charging consumers for a paid-download version.

On the other hand, if all of your competitors are charging up front for the app, it shows that your target audience is willing to pay in order to eliminate ads in their app.

You also want to look again at the apps you use most. Which ones did you spend money on up front? Which ones are you constantly making in-app purchases from? You want to figure out why you think there is enough value in either a paid download or in-app purchase to spend your money on it, and how your app can bring that same value.

While you are a small sample size, you also have perspective as an app user as to what makes you open your wallet. Are you more willing to pay up front? Do you shy away from in-app purchasing? Or do you like getting the app for free, testing it out, and then having the option to buy certain locked features of the app later?

Finally, check out the top-grossing apps to see how they are raking in money. Regardless of what they're offering, these apps are doing it right. See if there are trends you can spot across the most profitable apps.

Consumer preference is always changing, so it is important to tailor your app designs to what they want. Initially, most of the top-grossing apps were making their money from paid downloads. In recent years, however, there has been a shift in consumer preference to in-app purchasing. Apps like Candy Crush, Pandora, and Skype have consistently been among the highest-grossing apps by giving the app to mobile device users for free and then asking them to spend money as they use the app.

Ideally, you want your app to take advantage of these consumer trends. If one pricing strategy is clearly favored, you should try to develop your app with that in mind.

The apps that have already been developed are rich with data and information that can help you. The more you know about what works and what doesn't, the easier your design and programming stages are going to be. While you are eager to get started on building your app, it is critical that you spend some time learning more about the app marketplace so you can put yourself and your app in the best position to be a success.

Chapter Recap

Before you can actually start building your mobile app, you need to do a considerable amount of research on the app marketplace. You want to glean as much information as you can from those that have gone before you to learn from what they're doing right—and steer clear of what they're doing wrong. When you are researching the app marketplace, there are several things you must be looking for, including:

- Competitors: While there may not be other apps that do exactly what you envision for yours, there most likely is at least one that does something similar. Find out which apps would be considered your competitors by searching various keywords in various online app store search engines. Once you determine who else is in your app's space, you can see which ones are successful and determine how to make yours better.

- Design and functionality: When researching the app marketplace, you want to look not only at your competitors, but also at the apps you like and those that are highly rated to see what makes them worth buying. What is so great about the design and functionality of these apps? Take detailed notes on which apps have the best features and designs so you can apply those principles to your app during the design and programming stage.

- Pricing strategy: While studying the app marketplace for design and functionality, you should also be studying the pricing strategy of those same apps. You want to capitalize on the pricing strategy—paid download, in-app purchasing, or in-app advertising—that consumers are trending toward. Once you see which method consumers prefer, figure out a way to incorporate that monetization strategy into your app.

05

Registering as a Developer

Now that you have charted your course for success and researched the marketplace to ensure that you have a winning idea, it is time to make this venture official. That means registering as an app developer with Apple and Android, which lets operating system designers for both platforms know who you are and that you intend to start selling apps in their marketplaces. Because Apple and Android devices use different operating systems, it is necessary to register with both if you plan to sell your app to both sets of consumers. Those of you who plan to strictly use one or the other only need to register with that developer.

The process, which is relatively easy and inexpensive, offers app developers a number of things, including the developer tools needed to build apps, as well as a variety of support tools and documents that can help new developers fight through any difficulties they might encounter.

Becoming a Registered Apple Developer

If you are going to be developing an app to run on the iOS platform, you will first need to register as an Apple Developer. This process can be done online at https://developer.apple.com/register/index.action. When you visit that site, the first thing you will be asked to do is log in using your Apple ID. This is the same login used to log in to other Apple services, like iTunes and the Apple Online Store. If you already have an Apple ID, you can log in using that same ID and password. Those who are new to Apple and its services will need to create an Apple ID, which is one of the options provided on the initial developer registration.

Creating an Apple ID can also be done online via Apple's website. When you click on the "Create Apple ID" button on the developer page, you will automatically be redirected to the My Apple ID sign-up page. To get an ID, you will have to provide basic information about yourself, such as your name, birth date, and address. You will also select an Apple ID, which is generally your primary e-mail address, and a password. In addition, you will select a security question and answer so that you can retrieve your password if you lose it.

Once you have an Apple ID, you will return to the developer sign-up page and click on the "Sign In" button. The first thing you will be asked to do is review and "sign" Apple's Registered Apple Developer Agreement. The document outlines the relationship you will have with Apple, the benefits you will be provided, the restrictions you must adhere to, and the reasons that Apple can terminate you as a registered developer. While many people tend to gloss over agreements like this, I would suggest you read the document in its entirety. Apple will be a significant partner for developers who are creating apps solely to run on the iOS system, so it's important to know exactly what terms they will be holding you to.

Once you feel comfortable with the terms of the agreement, check the box at the bottom of the page. In lieu of an actual signature, clicking on the box and then clicking "Agree" confirms that you have read and agree to everything in the contract, and that you are legally considered an adult (i.e., eighteen or older) in your country of residence.

After you "sign" the agreement, the next page in the process will pop up. During this stage of the registration, you will be asked to tell Apple a little bit more about yourself and the apps you intend to create. The first two questions ask what role you have in developing the apps—such as designer, project manager, or software engineer—and when you started developing apps. Apple then asks more about what you are developing. This isn't a time to provide specifics, so talk in generalities. Because you have already done a thorough job of planning out the business, answering questions about the apps you plan to develop should be easy. Specifically, Apple wants to know if you're building an iOS app or an app for Mac computers using the OS X platform. It also asks you to list any other platforms for which you are currently developing, or have developed in the past. Once you answer those questions, click the "Register" button at the bottom of the page. By doing that, you are officially registered as an Apple developer.

By registering, you are now entitled to a number of resources designed to make the process of creating and selling mobile apps easier. The place you want to visit is the iOS Dev Center, which offers an array of technical resources, including the code needed to actually build an app. In addition to offering a download of the latest version of Xcode, the development center also includes documents to help you learn the fundamental concepts of iOS development, as well as videos featuring Apple experts talking about various aspects of developing mobile apps for the operating system. The iOS Dev Center also features a developer library where you can learn more about the technical aspects of creating apps on the iOS platform, and sample code to help you see all the features an app can include. If you plan to develop apps for either the

Legal Brief

One of the first things you will be asked to do when registering as an Apple or Android developer is agree to various marketplace developer agreements. Apple, Google, and all the other Android marketplaces have their own requirements and restrictions that developers must abide by. While the agreements, which require only a simple online check mark on your part, may seem standard, business attorney Jason Killips says that it is still extremely important to understand exactly what they contain.

"Just because something is standard doesn't make it good for you, so you should probably understand it before you begin work on your app. If you are going to put a lot of work into [your mobile app] and not be able to live with Apple's or Google's terms, maybe you don't want to get into this [business]," Killips says. "You want to make sure you know what those obligations are and take them into account from the very beginning."

Before sitting down with a lawyer, Killips says he would encourage mobile developers to search online to see what others have written about the agreement. Check to see if developers have run into issues with the agreement in the past. By simply spending some time online, Killips says you can get yourself pretty well versed in these types of online agreements.

"Doing some research will probably get you 80 percent of the way informed as to what you are dealing with," he says. "Should you still consult a lawyer? I probably would, because that way you can sit down and really explain what you are trying to do, and find out if there are any extra hiccups that you need to take into account. If you can't afford to do that, or are unable to do that for some reason at the outset, then just do the research and find some reputable sources."

Mac or the Safari web browser, there are separate development centers to log in to. They both offer similar features to the iOS Dev Center, including the code needed to start building an app.

While you are now registered as an Apple developer and have access to the tools needed to get started, you still will need to join the iOS Developer Program to develop the app, test it, and sell it. The program costs $99 a year and gives you access to the iOS Simulator, which lets you run, test, and debug your app on your home computer using a simulated iPhone or iPad, and the Interface Builder, which includes drag-and-drop design features. You will also be able to use Apple instruments to collect your app's performance data.

As a member of the iOS Developer Program, you can test the app on an iPhone, iPad, or iPod when you are finished with the development stage to see how it works in real time on the actual device it was built for. This also gives you the opportunity to see how the app performs when connected to a Wi-Fi or carrier's network. Because nothing works perfectly the first time, iOS Developer Program members also receive two chances to have actual Apple engineers offer guidance and code-level help to get your app working smoothly.

The final key service that comes with being a member of the iOS Developer Program is the ability to sell or distribute your app in the Apple App Store. Because the Apple App Store is the only place to legally buy apps for iPhones, iPads, and iPods, if you want to sell your app, you have no choice but to become a member of the Developer Program.

Joining the program is a simple process that can be done directly from your Apple home developer page. To join, you need to click "Programs & Add-ons" at the top of the page and then click the iOS Developer Program "Join Today" button on the following page. The next page, where you will now click "Enroll" at the top, describes all the features the program offers.

After signing in with your Apple ID, you must acknowledge whether you are working as an individual or company. If you choose "individual," your name will be listed as the seller of the app, and you will be the only one who has access to the program resources. If you select "company," your legal company name will be listed as the app seller, and you can have additional members of your team access the program's tools. Apple recommends that developers who hire outside contractors to build the apps for them enroll as a company and add the developers to their team.

While all you need is a credit card to join as an individual, to enroll as a company you will need to provide Apple with proof that you have the legal authority to bind your company to the Apple Developer Program legal agreements, as well as your company's D-U-N-S Number, which is a unique nine-digit number used as a standard business identifier. Once you have all that information, you can complete the enrollment process by agreeing to the license agreement and actually purchasing the program with your credit card. Within twenty-four hours of completing your purchase, you should receive an activation e-mail from Apple. Once you activate the program, you will have all the tools and resources needed to build, test, and sell your apps in the Apple App Store.

Becoming a Registered Android Developer

If you are choosing to release an Android mobile app, either solely on that platform or in addition to an iOS version, you need to register separately for that. Unlike developing apps for the Apple iOS, where registration is needed to access some of the critical tools necessary to building a successful app, Android developers can get those resources without registering first. To download all the developer design and testing tools, visit http://developer.android.com/tools/index.html. Once there, click on the "Download the Android SDK" link near the top of the page. Included in the Android developer tools is a development environment with advanced features to help build, test, debug, and package Android apps.

While you don't necessarily have to register as a developer with Android, you do have to register in the marketplaces in which you are going to sell. Unlike apps for iOS, which can only be sold in the Apple App Store, Android developers have a bit more freedom. While there are a variety of online marketplaces for Android apps, the two most popular with both consumers and developers are the Google Play and Amazon marketplaces. That is where you are going to want to initially register as a developer.

The Google Play Store

To register as a Google Play Android developer, you will need to visit https://play .google.com/apps/publish/v2/signup. Once there, you will be asked to sign in with your Google account login and password. Similar to Apple, if you are new to Google, you will first need to sign up for a login and password before enrolling in the developer program. If you need a Google account, click on the "Create a New Google Account" near the top of the page. Information you will need to provide to sign up for your Google account includes your first and last name, your username—which will also serve as your Google e-mail address—a password, birthday, gender, location, and current e-mail address. Even if you already have a personal account, Google recommends creating a new one for business purposes.

Once you have a Google login, you can continue enrolling in the Google Play Developer Console. However, before moving on, you must agree to the Google Play Developer distribution agreement. Like with Apple, this spells out the terms of the relationship you will have with Google. While standard and mandatory for all developers, I would recommend having someone skilled at reading a contract, possibly a lawyer family member or friend, explain exactly what you are agreeing to. After clicking on the box to agree, you have an opportunity to review all of the foreign countries, currently more than 130, in which you can distribute and sell your apps.

All that's left before really getting started is to pay your $25 registration fee. When you're ready to pay, click on the "Continue to Payment" button at the bottom of the page. A pop-up box will open asking you to set up a Google Wallet account, which stores your name and credit card number for future purchases. After entering your name, zip code, credit or debit card number, and the card's expiration date and security code, click the "Accept and Continue" link at the bottom of the box. You will have one more chance to review your purchase before officially paying the $25 registration fee.

Once your payment is approved, you will be asked to select a username to wrap up the Google Play developer registration process. As an official developer, you now have access to the tools you will need to start selling and managing your app in the Google Play marketplace.

The Amazon Appstore

In addition to the Google Play Store, many Android app developers choose to also sell their apps in the Amazon Appstore. To get your apps in the Amazon marketplace, which sells apps for the Kindle Fire tablets, you need to first register for the Amazon Mobile App Distribution Program. Enrolling in this program, which mirrors Apple's $99 annual fee, gives you all the tools needed to start selling your app to Kindle Fire users.

To register for the Amazon Mobile App Distribution Program, visit https://developer.amazon.com/welcome.html and click the "Create Account" link. To move forward, you must sign in with your Amazon login and password. If you don't have one, follow the steps provided to create a new one. After signing in, you will be asked to confirm some basic information about yourself, including name, address, and phone number.

Amazon next will have you agree to its Mobile App Distribution Agreement. Just like with Apple and Google, I would recommend having someone familiar with contracts read over the agreement so that you know exactly what it entails. Once you feel comfortable with the agreement, click on the "Continue" link at the bottom of the page.

Amazon then wants to know if you plan to sell your apps or just distribute them for free. Regardless of whether you charge for it up front or collect payments via in-app purchases, if you plan to monetize the apps at any point in the future, you must provide Amazon with some additional financial information (specifically, your banking details, including bank name and account numbers).

Because you will be making money off your apps, Amazon next has you complete its "Tax Identity Interview," which is designed to collect the necessary financial information—business status, tax status, and tax identification number—needed to complete IRS Forms W-9 or W-8BEN. Once Amazon has all that information, you can start selling your app in the Amazon marketplace.

■ ■ ■

Now that you've done your research, have a business plan, and are officially registered as a developer who can sell apps in the major Apple and Android marketplaces, it is time to start actually developing your first app.

Chapter Recap

Here is a recap of everything you need to register as an Apple and Android developer.

If you are registering as an Apple developer, you need:

- An Apple ID
- To provide basic personal information (name, address, birth date, etc.)
- To know what your role in the development process will be
- A legal company name if registering as a business
- Proof that you have the legal authority to bind your company to the Apple Developer Program legal agreements
- Your company's D-U-N-S Number
- $99 to pay the registration fee

If you are developing apps for Android and want to sell them in the Google marketplace, you need:

- A Google login
- A Google Wallet account
- Bank account details
- A completed IRS Form W-9 or W-8BEN
- $25 to pay the registration fee

If you are developing apps for Android and want to sell them in the Amazon Appstore, you need:

- An Amazon account
- Bank account details
- Tax status and identification number
- Completed IRS Form W-9 or W-8BEN
- $99 to pay the registration fee

06 | Building an App Yourself

The stage you have been waiting for is finally here. After extensive planning and research, it is finally time to turn that idea for an app into a reality. As we discussed in chapter 2, you have two options for building an app yourself: actually doing the coding and programming yourself, or using a do-it-yourself service.

Pros and Cons

Both options have their pros and cons. Developing apps on your own gives you ultimate and total control over every aspect of the project, including design features and timeline. You don't have to worry about the added struggle of trying to explain your vision to a developer who might not see things in the same light that you do. You want your finished app to look and operate just as you imagined and dreamed, and sometimes adding another person into the mix can make that difficult. By building it yourself, what you want is what you get. You also aren't restricted by a developer's timeline, which undoubtedly will be longer than you would like. When you build an app on your own, you only have yourself to blame if it doesn't get finished in a timely manner.

In addition, the low cost is a big plus for doing it without any outside help. Assuming you have a computer—and if you have programming experience, you most likely do—you can build mobile apps with the tools and developer environment that both Apple and Android provide to their developers. In fact, both can be downloaded for free before ever registering with Apple or Android.

However, while you might not have to shell out any money to develop apps on your own, it does come with a significant price. Programming an app is a very time-consuming process. Depending on the features included, it can take anywhere from a few weeks to eighteen months to build a ready-to-sell app. That means hours and hours of staring at a computer screen. If you have decided to do this on a full-time basis, the time commitment might not be as big of a factor as if you were working on this part-time. If this is an on-the-side venture, you must be prepared each day to leave one job, where you more than likely stare at a computer all day, to start work on another—your app business—doing the same thing.

Building apps on your own, without the help of a professional coder, is really only an option if you have programming experience. Without any knowledge of how programming works, you will be hard-pressed to learn everything needed to build a polished and professional-looking product. While most mobile app developers agree that building an app can be done with virtually any type of programming background, they also agree that you'd be better served by hiring someone if working with computer code isn't your forte.

The second option for building an app on your own is to use one of the numerous online do-it-yourself services. These online sites provide the templates and guides needed to build a working app—a good option for those with no programming knowledge. The main benefits of this route are time and money. With these services, apps can be built in just hours for less than $100.

That low price, however, means you get little control over the design and functionality of the app. By using a do-it-yourself service, you are severely limiting your design choices. The only options you have are from the provided templates, making it highly unlikely that your initial vision for the app will be realized in the final product. While each of the do-it-yourself services' apps can be customized for your needs, they all have the same basic look and feel. However, if you are hard-pressed for time and money, this might be your best bet.

Once you understand the pros and cons of each option, it is time to choose one and start moving forward, or to think about hiring someone else to handle this stage.

Programming for Apple iOS

If you have chosen to do all the programming and coding on your own, the first thing you'll want to do is get up to speed on developer environment, programming languages, and tools for the operating system on which you are going to be developing.

For those of you who decide to work on Apple's iOS platform, the two things you need to become most familiar with are Xcode and Objective-C. Xcode, Apple's developer environment, provides users with a workspace and all the tools needed to build and program a functioning mobile app for the iPhone, iPad, or Mac computer. Among the tools included in Xcode are:

- A source editor (complete with advanced code completion)
- Code folding
- Syntax highlighting and error warnings when code isn't lining up correctly
- A built-in interface builder that lets you design and test possible interfaces without having to write code for each one
- The iOS Simulator, which lets you use a Mac-based simulator to help build, install, run, and debug your app
- Static analysis, which finds problems in your code before you even get the app running

In all, Xcode offers users more than thirty-five features and tools to make the development process as smooth as possible.

Downloading the Apple Developer Tools

To start using Xcode, you can simply download it for free from the Mac App Store, which differs from the Apple App Store. After opening the Mac App Store, search for Xcode and click the "Free" link to start downloading. Once you provide your Apple username and password, the developer environment and tools will start downloading to your computer. The only requirement for running the latest version of Xcode is that your Mac computer is using at least OS X Lion (10.7) as an operating system.

Once the app is downloaded—which could take several minutes, or longer, depending on your Internet connection speed—you should open it and click the "Install" button to start installing the development application on your computer. After Xcode is downloaded and installed, you are ready to start programming.

While Xcode is the environment in which you work, Objective-C is the actual programming language needed to build a mobile app. The object-oriented language is what Apple requires developers to use when building mobile apps. According to Apple, Objective-C is a simple language with syntax and conventions that are easy to learn, especially for programmers who have worked with other object-oriented languages, such as Java or C++.

Regardless of whether you are a programming wizard or new to the game, I would highly suggest reading through some of the various Apple tutorials on how the language works. They include basic ones for those who are just getting started, as well as more-complex guides for programmers already at that next level. All of the tutorials are available for free on the Apple Developer website.

If you need a little help brushing up on or getting started using Xcode and Objective-C, there are numerous free online tutorials that Apple offers its developers. Some of those worth reading include:

- Write Objective-C Code: This helps users to become acquainted with Apple's primary programming language.
  https://developer.apple.com/library/ios/#referencelibrary/GettingStarted/RoadMapiOS/chapters/WriteObjective-CCode/WriteObjective-CCode/WriteObjective-CCode.html

- Acquire Foundational Programming Skills: The foundation toolkit for all iOS programming.
  https://developer.apple.com/library/ios/#referencelibrary/GettingStarted/RoadMapiOS/chapters/AcquireBasicProgrammingSkills/AcquireBasicSkills/AcquireBasicSkills.html

- Survey the Major Frameworks: A rundown of the frameworks most commonly used by iOS developers.
  https://developer.apple.com/library/ios/#referencelibrary/GettingStarted/RoadMapiOS/chapters/SurveytheMajorFrameworks/SurveytheMajorFrameworks/SurveytheMajorFrameworks.html

- Frameworks: This describes the kinds of methods found in Objective-C frameworks, and explains how you can integrate your app's code with a framework's code.
  https://developer.apple.com/library/ios/#referencelibrary/GettingStarted/RoadMapiOS/chapters/Frameworks.html

- Streamline Your App with Design Patterns: How to incorporate design patterns into your mobile app.
  https://developer.apple.com/library/ios/#referencelibrary/GettingStarted/RoadMapiOS/chapters/StreamlineYourAppswithDesignPatterns/StreamlineYourApps/StreamlineYourApps.html

- Design Your App with Care: Tips on how best to turn your idea into an app that will be appealing to users.
  https://developer.apple.com/library/ios/referencelibrary/GettingStarted/RoadMapiOS/chapters/DesignYourAppwithCare/DesignYourAppWithCare/DesignYourAppWithCare.html

- Know the Core Objects of Your App: This is a review of the UIKit—which provides the infrastructure for the app objects—and the role each plays.
  https://developer.apple.com/library/ios/#referencelibrary/GettingStarted/RoadMapiOS/chapters/KnowtheCoreObjectsofYourApp/KnowCoreAppObjects/KnowCoreAppObjects.html

- Internationalize Your App: Teaches you how to make your app available in multiple languages.
  https://developer.apple.com/library/ios/referencelibrary/GettingStarted/RoadMapiOS/chapters/InternationalizeYourApp/InternationalizeYourApp/InternationalizeYourApp.html

As someone who had years of programming experience but had never worked with Xcode or Objective-C, Kevin Hamilton says that he found them to be quite easy to learn when he was developing his Home Inventory app. Hamilton believes Apple's programming language and tools are easy to use for developers who may not have built a mobile app before, but have experience developing other types of software.

Hamilton, who has developed software for more than fifteen years, says he enjoys working with Apple's tools because they aren't overly complicated like other development tools and languages can be.

"I find them to be just the right balance of complexity and simplicity," Hamilton says. "They are right in the middle of what everyone else is doing. They give me just enough to solve the difficult problems, but they don't get in my way."

Programming for Android

Just like everything else with Android and Apple, the act of actually programming the apps is totally different. While an app may look exactly the same when used on an iPhone or Samsung Galaxy, it has actually been built completely differently from top to bottom.

Unlike with Apple, which uses Objective-C programming language, Android developers are required to use Java. Java is completely different from Objective-C, and requires a whole new set of skills and understanding to use. However, unlike Objective-C, which is used primarily for Apple development, Java has a much broader use, which means most developers have probably worked with it before. Not having to spend time learning a new language, as most have to do with Objective-C, is one significant reason that many developers start off with an Android app. Don't let that be a deciding factor, however, for why you choose to develop for Android. Though already knowing the ins and outs of Java might make developing the app a little easier, not being able to sell it in the Apple App Store could prove to be a big drawback if you're trying to make a profit. Be sure to base your platform decision on more than just your knowledge of one language over the other.

Android also has its own separate developer environment and tools. Titled Eclipse, the Android developer environment—like Apple's Xcode—features the workspace, tools, and support guides needed to build Android mobile apps. Among the developer tools included are:

- Template wizards to help you get started on new apps
- Static analysis capabilities that point out performance, usability, or correctness problems
- Options for developing on virtual devices, which lets you see how the app runs and performs on any hardware combination

In addition, there are powerful debugging and testing tools designed to ensure that your app reaches its optimum performance. Because he did have an extensive background in software development and web design, Alex Genadinik says he decided to build his first start-up business app on Android. His first app was designed to be solely a project to help him learn more about mobile app development.

What he found out was that even with his Java experience and knowing the basics of computer science and programming, it still took several weeks before he felt completely comfortable with what he was doing.

"It took me about a month and half from sitting down and coming up with the idea to launching my first version of the app, but that first version was really terrible," Genadinik says. "It was the most basic, basic thing. If this was a business, it wouldn't be launchable, but since this was just a project for me, I launched it. So it took about a month and half to get from zero to the worst possible app that you could imagine, but it was live. From there I picked things up pretty quickly."

Downloading the Android Developer Tools

The Android development tools can be downloaded for free, and without registration, by visiting http://developer.android.com/sdk/index.html. Once on the site, click the "Download the SDK" link on the right-hand side of the page. You then must agree to Android's terms and conditions before the downloading can proceed. Over the next few minutes, the Android "ADT Bundle" will be downloaded to your PC. When the download is complete, you need to install the software by first unpacking the Zip file, called "adt-bundle," which will most likely be located in your computer's "Downloads" file. You need to move the file out of the download file and save it to a different part of your computer, such as the desktop. Once you do that, you can click on the Eclipse file, titled "adt-bundle-<os_platform>/eclipse/," to start developing your apps.

Before you jump into your project, it would be advisable to spend some time reviewing the various Android help and support tutorials. From step-by-step guides for beginners to best-practice lessons for developers with more-complex needs, there is most likely an Android tutorial that will have your answer.

Online Resources: Android Tutorials

Android offers a wide range of tutorials and guides to help developers work through issues they might be facing. Some of the most helpful guides include:

- Getting Started: Tips on building your first app, managing the activity life cycle, supporting different devices, building a dynamic user interface (UI) with fragments, saving data, interacting with other apps, and sharing content.
  http://developer.android.com/training/index.html

- Building Apps with Multimedia: Tips on managing audio playback and capturing photos.
  http://developer.android.com/training/building-multimedia.html

- Building Apps with Graphics & Animation: Tips on displaying bitmaps efficiently, displaying graphics with OpenGL ES, and adding animations.
  http://developer.android.com/training/building-graphics.html

- Building Apps with Connectivity & the Cloud: Tips on connecting devices wirelessly, performing network operations, transferring data without draining the battery, and syncing to the cloud.
  http://developer.android.com/training/building-connectivity.html

- Building Apps with User Info & Location: Tips on accessing contacts data, remembering users, and making your app location aware.
  http://developer.android.com/training/building-userinfo.html

- Best Practices for User Experience & UI: Tips on designing effective navigation, implementing effective navigation, notifying the user, adding search functionality, designing for multiple screens, designing for TV, creating custom views, creating backward-compatible UIs, and implementing accessibility.
  http://developer.android.com/training/best-ux.html

- Best Practices for User Input: Tips on using touch gestures and handling keyboard input.
  http://developer.android.com/training/best-user-input.html

- Best Practices for Performance: Tips for improving layout performance, running in a background service, loading data in the background, optimizing battery life, sending operations to multiple threads, and keeping your app responsive.
  http://developer.android.com/training/best-performance.html

- Best Practices for Security & Privacy: Tips on security with HTTPS and SSL.
  http://developer.android.com/training/best-security.html

Whether it's Apple or Android, the rest of the building is up to you. How complex it is, how long it takes, and how well the finished product turns out is all on your shoulders. If your programming experience is little or nonexistent, and reading more about Objective-C and Java has made you more baffled than enlightened, you do have another option if you are determined to build your apps yourself.

Using a Do-It-Yourself Service

There are a number of online outlets that offer do-it-yourself mobile app building services. These services, such as TheAppBuilder and AppMakr, provide ready-made templates to get you started. The only work you need to do is to customize your vision by adding the features and text you need. Building the app is easily done through a simple drag-and-drop approach that makes building an app a possibility for those with no programming or coding experience.

The major benefits to choosing a do-it-yourself app builder are costs and time. Unlike hiring a developer—which can cost anywhere from $1,000 to $10,000 for a freelancer, or $25,000 to $100,000 for a digital agency—do-it-yourself app builders

Online Resources: Mobile App Building Services

There is a wide range of online do-it-yourself mobile app building services. They provide you with the basic templates and tools needed to build an app, without the need for any programming experience. Some of the do-it-yourself services include:

- ANZ Hosting: www.anzhosting.com
- AppBreeder: www.appbreeder.com
- appsbar: www.appsbar.com
- AppsBuilder: www.apps-builder.com/en/home
- BuildAnApp: www.buildanapp.com
- iBuild App: http://ibuildapp.com
- Make me Droid: www.makemedroid.com/en
- Mippin: http://mippin.com
- Mobincube: www.mobincube.com
- TheAppBuilder: www.theappbuilder.com

are just a fraction of the cost. Most of the apps can be built for less than $100. In addition, they can be finished in days, compared to either coding it yourself or using an outside developer, which can take anywhere from four to eighteen months.

The major drawback of using such a service is that you risk losing much of your creative vision, and most likely the app you have been imagining will not be the finished product you end up with. While these services do produce professional-looking apps, they are very stripped down in terms of features and interface options. In the end, these apps tend to be less desirable to consumers. If you are choosing this option strictly because of cost considerations, you might want to reconsider. While this is a cheaper option than hiring a freelance developer from a digital agency to build the app, it isn't necessarily the most cost-effective. Although your initial investment may be small, if consumers aren't interested, the return is going to be even smaller. In the end, you may want to hold off on the programming stage until you can raise enough money to hire someone who can produce an app that not only looks professional, but is also high-functioning enough to get smartphone and tablet users to buy it.

If you don't feel comfortable coding yourself or investing in a do-it-yourself service that may or may not produce the app you are picturing, you really need to consider forgoing plans of building it yourself. Instead, you may be better suited for putting your efforts and resources toward hiring a professional freelancer or digital agency to do all of the programming for you.

Chapter Recap

Here is a recap of the questions you need to be asking yourself to determine whether your skill sets are best suited for building your own mobile app without the help of any professional programmers:

1. Do you have any programming experience with any type of software?

While you don't have to be an expert in the Apple or Android programming languages to build your own app, it does make the process much easier if you have experience in computer programming of any sort. If you have never coded or programmed any software, you need to be prepared to spend a lot of time learning how to do so if you are determined to build it on your own.

2. Have you ever worked specifically with Objective-C?

Even with prior programming experience, if you haven't worked specifically with Apple's programming language, Objective-C, you will need to learn all the ins and outs of this platform before you can really get started.

3. Have you ever worked specifically with Java?

If Android is the platform you are working with, then you need to know all there is to know about Java. Past programming experience might help you with the overall concept of coding a mobile app, but unless you understand Java specifically, you won't be able to get very far in the building process.

4. Can you commit the massive amount of time needed to program a mobile app?

Building your own mobile app requires hours and hours of time sitting in front of your computer. If you don't want to make that investment, you may need to consider scrapping plans to build apps by yourself.

5. Are you ready to give up control of design and functionality by choosing a do-it-yourself service?

When using these online services, you are limited to using only their provided templates and features. While these services are cheaper and faster, they offer little in terms of design creativity.

07 Building an App with the Help of a Developer

The good news for those who either don't know much about computer programming or really don't want the hassle of dealing with it is that there are many people out there willing—for the right price—to do it for you. When hiring a professional programmer, the first choice you need to make is whether you plan to use a freelancer or a larger digital agency.

Pros and Cons

Hiring an outside programmer has its benefits and drawbacks. First and foremost is the cost. Depending on the programmer you use and what you expect of them and your finished product, it can be quite pricey to hire someone from the outside. In the end, your choice will come down, at least in part, to finances. If you have the money to spend, you will be much happier with what a digital agency can provide. However, that being said, there are a number of very talented freelancers who can give you what you want for a cheaper price. The hard part is finding the right one. Let's take a closer look at some of the pros and cons of each option.

Freelancers

If you use a freelancer, you can expect to work with one person—most likely, someone from overseas—who will handle all aspects of the programming, coding, debugging, and testing on his or her own. If you want to go with an independent freelance programmer based overseas, costs can range between $1,000 and $5,000. The price is significantly higher—$20,000 to $500,000—if you decide to go with an app development agency in the United States.

In addition to the added expense of hiring an outside programmer, you give up some control over the app. Instead of knowing exactly where the app stands at all times, you must rely on regular status updates to understand how much progress has been made. What you have to remember is that no matter how much you are paying them, you will always have more invested in this than the programmer will. Regardless of whether it is a freelancer from Elance.com or a Manhattan-based digital agency, they won't be working on your project around the clock. It will be one of possibly many that they are working on concurrently, which means your app isn't getting their undivided attention. For those without programming experience, the major benefit to hiring an outside developer is that the finished product will surely be more professional and appealing to consumers than what you would likely be able to produce on your own.

Freelancers are by far the cheaper of the two outside programmer options. While prices for a mobile app project always depend on the features and capabilities you're looking for, freelancers typically charge between $1,000 and $7,500 to build a fully functional and consumer-ready mobile app.

Digital Agencies

A digital agency, on the other hand, is typically equipped with a team of employees who specialize in different aspects of the project, such as programming, graphics, and connectivity. However, with that added team of specialists comes an increased cost. Expect to pay tens of thousands of dollars to work with a digital agency, but also know that in the end, you will probably be getting a much more professional, polished, and functional mobile app.

As with freelancers, your app won't be the only project the digital agency is working on. However, unlike a freelancer, who is just one person, a digital agency has a whole staff of people available to program your app at any given time. So while not everyone will always be focused on your app, in most cases there is at least one person working on it at all times.

Hiring a Freelance Developer

If your budget limits you to a freelancer, you need to start immediately on what can be a rather extensive mission to find one. Because there are so many mobile app freelancers, it is important to find the right person who will work with you to make sure you get what you want. However, be prepared: The marketplace is full of those who promise the world but can't ever live up to those guarantees. You need to conduct thorough interviews to get the scoop on their programming experience and feel out what they're really like to work with. This is, after all, someone with whom you'll be working closely for at least several months. You want to make sure you mesh not only on a professional level, but on a personal level as well. Make sure that your personalities are compatible so that you can work together effectively.

Freelance Marketplace Websites

To find a freelancer, you can visit one of the numerous online freelance marketplace websites. Sites like Elance.com and Freelancer.com are for professionals of any sort looking to hire outside help for a variety of different projects, such as writers, marketers, and designers. You can find thousands of mobile developers on these sites, each with different backgrounds and skill levels. These sites provide a perfect opportunity to match up developers like you, who have an idea for an app but don't know how to build it, with professional programmers looking for work.

There is a cost to using these online sites, however. Each site collects a commission for each match it successfully makes. For example, Elance gets an 8.75 percent commission when the project is finished. To protect you, the majority of these sites

Online Resources: Freelance Developers

There are thousands of freelance mobile app developers looking to work with people just like you. Here are some online sites to get you started on the process of finding a freelance mobile app developer:

- AppBooker: www.appbooker.com
- Elance: www.elance.com/r/contractors/q-Mobile/cat-it-programming/ind-true
- Freelancer: www.freelancer.com/work/freelance-mobile-app-developer
- Freelancers Outpost: www.freelancersoutpost.com/freelance-mobile-app -development-jobs
- GetAppQuotes: www.getappquotes.com
- Girapps: http://girapps.com/
- Mobileappfreelance: http://mobileappfreelance.com
- oDesk: https://www.odesk.com/
- NewAppIdea: www.newappidea.com

employ escrow accounts where the money for the project is stored until the project is finished. They give you the option of paying the programmer by the hour, or at a fixed rate for the entire project. The freelancers only receive money from the escrow account once they meet certain project milestones.

These freelancers are from all over the world. In fact, the majority of the mobile programmers on freelance job sites are based overseas. That shouldn't scare you off, however. Even if the freelancer was located in the United States, the likelihood that you would actually work with them face-to-face is slim. On projects like this, all the communication can be done online, either through e-mail or instant chats. Today's technology makes it just as easy to work with someone on the outskirts of Beijing as it is to work with a freelancer next door. Price is a key reason why many developers enjoy working with international developers, as many offer the same services as domestic developers at much cheaper prices.

While each freelance job site is different, the steps needed to use them are fairly similar. You first need to register as a developer, which is free on most sites, and gives you the ability to start searching for a developer who meets your criteria. Once you are signed in, you have the option to either browse the different available freelancers or send out a "job posting" to let the freelancers know about your project.

When browsing the freelancer listings, you need to first search by category and filter out those who aren't mobile developers. For the mobile developers that remain, you can review their bios, which include: their specialties, such as Android or iOS; information on past work experience; how many jobs they have had; their site rating, which is based on reviews from users who have worked with them in the past; and basic pricing information. After reviewing the bios and finding some developers who might be a good match, you can contact them directly through the site to continue your interview process.

Job Postings

The second option is to fill out a job posting and let the freelancers contact you if they are interested in the project. When posting your job, you want to provide enough information so that the mobile freelance developers will understand what you need, but not so much detail that someone could easily steal your idea. In the job posting, for example, you can give a brief idea of the type of app it will be, such as a game or a photo app, as well as the platform (Apple or Android) and the devices (smartphones or tablets) you'd like it to run on. You can then provide specifics on the level of experience you want your developer to have, as well as a request for examples of past work when developers respond to your posting. You then set a time limit, anywhere from a few days to a few weeks, for how long the developers have to "apply" for your job.

Instead of listing all of the specific skills you want your programmer to have, Lee (see below) advises keeping it simple by listing only iOS or Android programming

Expert's View: Choosing a Freelancer

Tim Lee

Former English as a Second Language teacher Tim Lee says he turned to oDesk to find a freelance programmer, and he learned a quick lesson about being too specific when he received only a smattering of responses to his first ad.

After posting several ads, the twenty-five-year-old Lee started asking the developers to send him past apps they'd worked on to see what they looked like and how they performed, and conducted background checks on Google using their username. If those checked out, he held online chat interviews with the freelance programmers to get a better feel for their personality and work style. It was those initial online chats that Lee says he put a lot of stock in.

"I was just asking simple questions to get a feel for how quickly they could respond and get a basic conversation going, to see how well I gelled with the guy," Lee says. "Any little feelings that this guy wasn't being too straight with me [made me feel that it] wasn't worth it for me. If they can't even do this interview, what is it going to be like when they work on the game?"

Lee says he'd advise newbies in the business to not rush this stage of the app development process. While you are undoubtedly eager to get the ball rolling, he says, you want to make sure the person you hire can deliver what you need, and expect.

"I took this very, very seriously," Lee says. "My motto was basically, hire slow, fire fast. It took me, like, two and half months to finally find someone. I think I had eight different want ads. Finally, someone wrote to me, and I got a good feeling from him right away. In the interview he answered me quickly, and we had a good back-and-forth. It was stuff like this that made me want to choose this guy. He was punctual, his portfolio looked good, and I just had a good feeling about him. It turned out to be one of the best decisions I have ever made."

knowledge as a skill requirement, depending on the platform you'd like to work on. This widens the pool of programmers, giving you more options to find the best match.

Whether you are reaching out to freelancers or posting a job ad, the next step is to wait and see who responds. What you don't want to do is jump on the first freelancer who gets back to you. It is important to give the process some time so that everyone who wants to respond can do so. Once you have a field of candidates, it is critical to conduct as thorough an interview as possible to ensure that you get the right person.

Because many freelancers will apply for the job without reading what you are looking for, one trick is to include a clause in your job description that asks them to use a certain keyword in the first line of the response so you know they were paying attention. For example, you can write in the job posting, "If after reading the job description you feel as if your skills are a good fit, please respond by including the words 'I was paying attention' in the first line of your response to confirm that you did in fact read my job posting in its entirety."

Choosing the Right Freelancer

Once you have a collection of potential hires, there are a number of factors you want to take into consideration when attempting to choose freelancers who would be a good match for you. First and foremost, it is critical to look at their past work. They could be friendly, easy-to-work-with people, but if their skills aren't up to par, that doesn't mean a thing. Ask those you are interested in to send you examples of other apps they have designed and programmed. By playing around with their work, you can get a feel for how experienced and polished their skills are.

Check out their user ratings, and read feedback from past clients to see if anything good or bad sticks out. You can always reach out to some of their past clients directly to ask what the freelancers were like to work with, how responsive they were, whether they indeed met their deadlines, and whether they delivered what they promised.

Eventually, you can take the process to the next level by conducting actual interviews. Because in-person interviews will be hard to accomplish, use an online chat service like Skype to ask more questions and get a better feel for the person. Ask questions about their work ethic, past projects, and some more personal questions to see if this person is someone you think you can easily work with to realize your dream.

When developing his SuChef app, Manne Darby, a member of the US Navy who is currently employed full-time by the Department of Defense, worked with two

How I Did It

Benny Hsu, Photo 365

Mobile developer Benny Hsu—who has launched several mobile apps, including Photo 365—says that while sites like Elance.com and oDesk.com are perfect for those who have a strong desire to get into the mobile app industry, but have little or no programming experience, they also make things challenging. This is because it is up to you to filter through the thousands of developers, each with his or her own range of skills.

Hsu turned to app development in 2011 after trying every way under the sun to make money online. From niche websites and blogging to an eBay business and affiliate marketing, Hsu tried and failed to turn a profit each and every time. His interest in mobile apps was piqued when he saw how popular they were becoming, but he was hesitant to join the industry because of his lack of programming knowledge. After doing a little investigation, he realized there were plenty of others just like him, with no mobile experience, making money off apps by having someone else build them. After reading about the success others had found using a professional freelancer, he decided he couldn't pass up the opportunity. In January 2011, he posted his first ad on Elance for a mobile developer that could help him realize his idea for a photo app.

It took no time at all for signs of interest to start rolling in.

"I just said I was looking for someone who was hardworking, had patience—because it was my first app—and good communication, and then I posted it," Hsu says of his job posting. "I got a whole bunch of replies, and I just started going through each one to see if any of them caught my attention and seemed like it would be a good fit."

Hsu spent time checking out the portfolios of those who responded and reading through feedback from past clients to see what their experience had been like. For the ones who measured up, Hsu took the hiring process to a second stage.

"I sent them a message to ask them some basic questions," Hsu says. "I wanted to see how quickly they responded, and how their communication was. Were they willing to help me answer my questions, or were they just really short with me?"

Hsu continued e-mailing with the potential developers to get a better feel for each before ultimately narrowing his list to a final three. It wasn't until then that he started talking specifics, including how much the project would cost and how long it would take.

(Continued on next page)

Hsu was quoted between $1,000 and $4,000 to program and design his Photo 365 mobile app, which helps users save a photo a day for a year.

"I finally found a [freelancer] out of Ukraine that I decided to hire," he says. "He wasn't the most expensive, he wasn't the cheapest, but he was one that I thought would be a good fit, and would build my app the way I wanted to."

In the end, Hsu said his hard work paid off as he found a developer that he had a good working relationship with and who produced the type of quality work he was looking for.

different freelancers—both of whom he found on Elance—and experienced two different working styles.

Because the app, which helps users come up with recipes based on the food they have in their pantry, required an extensive database, Darby decided it would be more efficient to have two different freelancers work on his project at the same time: one who focused on programming the app, and another who worked solely on the app's database, which was needed to house the app's recipes and ingredients list.

One way Darby determined whether a freelancer was going to be a good fit was not to hire the person for the whole project at first. Instead of farming out the whole job from the beginning for thousands of dollars, he says, first-time developers should have freelancers work on smaller, less-expensive projects to see the kind of work they produce and the manner in which they do so.

For example, he suggests that you consider outsourcing the work on just the wireframing—an outline of what the app will look like and a job done typically for between $500 and $1,000—to gauge freelancers' work, and whether or not you think you could have positive working relationships with them. This way, he says, you aren't throwing all of your money at one person whom you aren't truly sure will get the job done in the end.

"It is a learning process to feel out who is going to do the best job," Darby says.

It is important to trust your gut during this stage. Even if a portfolio seems great and past clients have raved about the person's work ethic, if you get a bad vibe during the interview, don't be scared to move on to someone else. You will be working with this freelancer for months at a time, and you don't want to waste your money, or your (or their) time.

If you're concerned with the risks associated with working with a freelancer and money isn't an object, your needs may be best served by hiring a digital agency.

Hiring a Digital Agency

The same basic principles used to hire a freelancer are used in hiring a digital agency. Their past work, client recommendations, work style, cost, and timeline all need to be investigated. While you might think the risk of working with a digital agency isn't as great as hiring an unknown freelancer from halfway across the globe, that's not necessarily the case because of the costs involved. Some consider the risk even greater because the amount of money being invested is considerably more.

The job of finding an agency falls on your shoulders. Fortunately, there are online sites to help facilitate your connection. Some websites, like Best Web Design Agencies and SourcingLine, offer reviews and rankings for dozens of agencies. While these lists may provide you with a starting point, there are many other firms doing excellent work that aren't included for one reason or another.

One way to wade through the digital agencies is to study some of the apps you like best—not just the ones you have the most fun using, but the ones that have the best graphics, the easiest user interface, and the most complex features. While the digital agency that built the app probably won't be found on the seller's page in the Apple

Online Resources: Digital Agencies

There are several online sites designed specifically to help you wade through the numerous digital agencies with mobile app experience. These sites offer rankings, reviews, and portfolios of dozens of digital agencies in the United States and abroad. Among them:

- Agency Spotter: www.agencyspotter.com
- Award Winning Agencies Database: www.awardwinninginteractiveagencies.com
- Best Web Design Agencies: www.bestwebdesignagencies.com
- FabHire: www.fabhire.com
- SourcingLine: www.sourcingline.com
- Top Interactive Agencies: www.topinteractiveagencies.com

App Store or Google Play marketplace, you can click through to their website, where, with a little digging, you should be able to find the app's programmer.

If it's not there, don't hesitate to send app sellers a short note saying how much you enjoy their app, and asking if they used a digital agency—and, if so, which one. This is also a quick way to gauge if app sellers were happy with the agencies they worked with. If they write back with a name, don't be shy about following up with some more questions about the process, the company's working style, and how happy the seller was with the overall experience. Once you have a collection of digital agencies you want to check out, visit their websites to get more details before contacting them. On their site, you should be able to get a better picture of the type of company they are, the style of apps they specialize in, and some examples of mobile apps they've built in the past.

Whether it's by using online ranking and review sites, studying your favorite mobile apps, or even just doing some simple Google searches, it's helpful to find anywhere from ten to twenty agencies—not just one or two—that you feel are worth contacting and investigating further. Part of the reason: Not all of them are going to be interested in working with you. Well-established digital agencies might be less willing to work with someone who has no experience in the mobile app industry, and smaller shops might not have the time to take on your programming needs immediately. There are a host of reasons why a digital agency wouldn't want to work with you. Put a substantial list together with the mind-set that any of the choices could be a good match.

The next step is to start reaching out to them. While e-mail is always an option, a phone call is the best way to get immediate results. When you call, give some brief details about who you are, and mention that you are looking to hire a firm that can build you a mobile app. At this point, the firms that aren't interested or don't have time will likely stop you and let you know it's best for you to focus your efforts somewhere else.

Choosing the Right Digital Agency

When you find an agency willing to work with you, don't just sign up. As with hiring a freelancer, you need to conduct thorough interviews with representatives of these agencies to ensure that they have the necessary skills to build your app, and a working style that will mesh with yours. Instead of using this time to talk about what you are looking for in terms of your app's specifics, use it to study as much as you can about each agency. The beginning of this interview process should be all about them and what they bring to the table.

Among the specific questions you want to ask them:

- Do they specialize in one platform over another?
- Do they focus on certain types of apps?
- Who are some of their past clients?
- How long did each project take?
- How often will they communicate back and forth, and in what format—e-mail, Skype, instant messaging, phone call, etc.?

Also ask to see samples of the apps they've built, and request that they show some specific examples of the more-impressive features they have added to each. Determine whether or not the apps they've built in the past have the type of professional look you want and an easy-to-use interface.

Everything from the typeface and graphics to the loading time and performance should be top-notch. Because you will inevitably be paying a lot more for a digital agency than a freelancer, you should expect a lot more from them. If the agency doesn't have exactly what you are looking for, move on to the next one on your list.

In addition to learning more about each agency's specific talents, it is important at this point to determine whether you like the company's working style. Whether you prefer a more laid-back approach or an agency that's more formal, the agency you choose should fit the bill. Because you will be working so closely with them, picking an agency with a culture that doesn't mesh with what you're expecting can be a recipe for certain app development disaster.

Throughout this first interview, it's best to not share too many details about your app idea. Talk in generalities about the type of app it is and the features you want it to include. If you are not too specific about the app's details, you don't have to worry about having every developer you contact sign a nondisclosure agreement, which ensures that the digital agency won't share your app idea with anyone else.

Once you have trimmed down your list to the digital agencies that have the ability to produce the mobile app you desire and mesh with your style, you can start negotiating a deal.

How I Did It

Caroline Fielding, Bus Rage App

Single mom and part-time mobile app developer Caroline Fielding wasted little time trying to find a digital agency to program her Bus Rage app. Less than twenty-four hours after the idea came to her, Fielding was on the phone, calling a dozen different digital agencies around the country that she had found online.

"The next day I started calling around to different developers," says Fielding, who discovered through the process that only about half of the twelve she called were willing to work with her. "About 30 percent of them never called me back at all, and some called back and said they would not sign a nondisclosure agreement. So, they were out, because it's an idea they can basically steal from you, and you want to protect yourself."

Fielding then spent some time doing her own investigation into the companies that were willing to work with her.

"I looked at their website, I checked with the Better Business Bureau, Consumer-Reports.com, Ripoff Report, that kind of thing," she says. "I just did a little bit of due diligence."

She then talked to the different companies to learn more about their fees, the length of time they thought it would take to finish programming the app, their customer service, and their professionalism.

For Fielding, a Florida resident, California-based Avenue Social was the perfect match. The digital agency, which has developed numerous mobile app games, as well as mobile apps for businesses such as Jiffy Lube and P.F. Chang's, handled every technical aspect of building Fielding's Bus Rage game. For their work—which took fourteen months, and included several updates after Bus Rage was finished and released in the Apple App Store—Fielding says she paid roughly $35,000.

What impressed her most was the agency's responsiveness and innovative mind-set.

"They are actually quite wonderful, and I am using them for my second app right now," Fielding says. "We had weekly conference calls and back-and-forth e-mails, and sometimes they'd come up with ideas that I would have never even thought of, like linking a Facebook page with my app."

Negotiating a Contract

Whether you are working with a freelancer or a digital agency, once you find candidates that you're comfortable working with, it is time to start talking specifics. Now is the time to share a little bit more about your idea so that the developer can start figuring out how much it is going to cost and how long it is going to take. Because you will be talking in more detail and you don't want anyone to steal your ideas, you would be best served to have anyone you are negotiating with sign a standard nondisclosure agreement.

Nondisclosure Agreements

Nondisclosure agreements are legal documents that protect your mobile app idea. Having a freelancer or digital agency sign a nondisclosure agreement helps to ensure that they don't take your concept and either develop it themselves or share it with someone else. By not requiring programmers to sign a nondisclosure agreement, you are running the risk that they will pass on working with you, steal the idea for themselves, program the app quickly, and rush it into the marketplace before yours is ready to be sold. Beating you to the marketplace could sink your app, and your business, in a heartbeat.

Specifically, a nondisclosure agreement spells out exactly which information will be considered protected and confidential, and the terms for how long it shall be kept secret. Because nondisclosure agreements are rather common in the mobile app industry, you shouldn't have much trouble getting a digital agency to agree to sign and abide by one. These are professional companies that build their reputation around not only doing outstanding work, but also developing relationships with clients based on trust. With so many digital agencies out there, those that are stealing ideas will quickly gain a negative reputation and see themselves out of business shortly thereafter.

Freelancers, however, could be a different story. One problem with working with freelancers overseas is that even if they do violate a nondisclosure agreement, it would be hard to bring them to justice for it. Conducting an international legal battle over a mobile app is something few are willing, or financially able, to take on. This comes back to trusting your gut. If you have the slightest bit of angst or reservation about working with a freelancer you're interviewing, keep looking for someone else.

While your best option is to have a lawyer draft a nondisclosure agreement for you and your work specifically, there are a number of sample agreement templates

Here is an example of what a nondisclosure agreement may look like. This should not be used as an actual legal contract, but it gives you an idea of what one might contain.

MUTUAL NONDISCLOSURE AGREEMENT

This Mutual Nondisclosure Agreement (the "Agreement"), effective as of _____ (the "Effective Date"), is agreed to between _____ and _____. The parties are engaged in _____ (the "Project"), and anticipate disclosing certain information to each other as part of that effort. The purpose of this agreement is to maintain the confidentiality of that information.

1. Confidential Information. All information disclosed by one party (the "Disclosing Party") to the other (the "Receiving Party") or to Receiving Party's agents, advisors, affiliates, or employees (collectively, "Receiving Party's Agents") that relates to the Project is "Confidential Information" and within the scope of this Agreement, subject only to the exclusions below. (Both the Disclosing Party and the Receiving Party include each party's agents, advisors, affiliates, or employees.)

2. Covenant of Nondisclosure. Receiving Party will hold in strict confidence and not disclose to any person any Confidential Information without the prior written consent of Disclosing Party. Receiving Party agrees to limit the use of the Confidential Information to the Project, and may not use any Confidential Information for any other purpose. Receiving Party will take all reasonable steps to preserve the confidentiality of the Confidential Information and prevent its disclosure to third parties, including but not limited to limiting the access to the Confidential Information to those of Receiving Party's agents, advisors, affiliates, or employees that require access to the Confidential Information for purposes of the Project.

3. Exclusions. This Agreement does not apply to information: 1) that at the time of disclosure was generally available to and known by the public (other than as a result of a disclosure by Receiving Party or an unauthorized or unlawful disclosure by any other person); 2) that was already known to Receiving Party at the time of Disclosing Party's disclosure; 3) that became available to Receiving Party on a nonconfidential basis from a source other than Disclosing Party, provided that the source of the information was not bound by a confidentiality agreement with or other contractual, legal, or fiduciary obligation of confidentiality to Disclosing Party; or 4) that is developed by Receiving Party independent of any information provided by Disclosing Party. Receiving Party may disclose Confidential Information as may be required by law, upon five days' prior written notice to Disclosing Party.

4. Return of Information. Upon the written request of Disclosing Party, Receiving Party will promptly deliver to Disclosing Party all Confidential Information Receiving Party has acquired, and destroy all memoranda, notes, reports, and documents, and all copies thereof, regardless of the medium in which the Confidential Information is stored, prepared by Receiving Party from the Confidential Information.

5. Remedies. Receiving Party acknowledges that it will be difficult to measure accurately the damages to Disclosing Party resulting from any breach by Receiving Party of the covenants and restrictions set forth in this Agreement, and that damages would not be an adequate remedy for any injury to Disclosing Party from any such breach. Therefore, Receiving Party agrees that Disclosing Party will be entitled to equitable relief, including injunction and specific performance, in the event of any breach or threatened breach of the provisions of this Agreement, in addition to all other remedies available to Disclosing Party at law or equity.

6. Applicable Law. This Agreement is to be governed, in all respects, by the laws of the State of Illinois.

It is so agreed:

[Party 1 name]   **[Party 2 name]**

_____   _____
(Signature)

_____   _____
(Print Name)

_____   _____
(Title)

_____   _____
(Date)

online that are available for those without access to an attorney. With the templates, you can quickly insert specifics about yourself and your app to complete the agreement. Once you tailor the agreement to fit your needs, send it off for them to sign.

A Legal Brief

When you are ready to start talking specifics with either a freelance programmer or a digital agency, Michigan attorney Jason Killips advises mobile app developers to always use a nondisclosure agreement.

Killips says that the legal contract is a way for two parties to share information with each other that they want kept secret. In addition to keeping the information—such as an idea for a mobile app—secret, nondisclosure agreements ensure that the protected information can't be used for any other purpose. This means that freelance programmers who sign nondisclosure agreements can't steal your app ideas and develop them on their own.

"It is a way for companies or individuals to have some confidence sharing important, private information with one another so they can talk freely and explore partnerships and work together, without risk that they are sharing these secrets with the entire industry and the entire world," he says.

Killips believes nondisclosure agreements are especially critical for mobile developers, because a mobile app idea can end up being just as valuable as the end product.

"We are talking about ideas, and the idea is the money," Killips says. "That is your valuable product. If you have an idea for the next Flipboard or for a good Twitter client or a great game, you don't want to give that to a programmer who says, 'That's a good idea, but if I make this one little change it is even better. So [the] heck with this [developer], I'm going to go off and design and market this on my own.' If your currency is ideas, then you have to do everything you can to protect those ideas."

Killips warns mobile app developers to be hesitant about working with programmers—either freelancers or digital agencies—who refuse to sign a nondisclosure agreement. If you do run across a programmer who is against signing, though, Killips suggests that you should find out why before discarding that person.

"A lot of times, the reason someone is unwilling to sign can be addressed," he says. "A lot of those objections, just by talking back and forth through the issues, can be resolved. If, on the other hand, you have someone who just says, 'I'm not signing [nondisclosure agreements],' I'm probably not going to do business with them."

When working with a freelance programmer from overseas, Killips advises developers to have them sign a nondisclosure agreement, too—even though it might not help you very much in a court of law. For example, if you are working with a programmer in Singapore who steals your idea and gives it to someone else to develop, Killips says a signed nondisclosure agreement probably can't help you that much.

"The ability to enforce these things overseas, both from a legal and a practical perspective, can be quite limited," Killips says. "Realistically, the guy probably doesn't have any money, so he is not worth suing anyway. And the expense of hiring counsel in Singapore to prosecute this guy is going to be cost-prohibitive, given what you will probably get in return. So from that standpoint, you probably are not going to get a great deal out of these things."

Regardless, he believes there are some big benefits to having the agreement signed. First and foremost, he says that it is a sign of trust, and the next best thing to looking someone in the eye and shaking on a deal.

"When you are dealing with people overseas, or even three towns over, but you can't get together to shake hands on it, putting pen to paper has a similar effect," Killips says. "It is more likely your programmer is going to abide by your confidentiality agreement if he has signed an NDA. There is just sort of an extra honesty factor."

A signed nondisclosure agreement could also help persuade Apple, Google, or any of the other Android marketplaces to stop the app from ever being sold. A signed legal document could be enough to show them that this programmer was in clear violation of your agreement.

"I don't know if you will win that, but I know you'll have a heck of a better case if you have a signed NDA," he says.

Once you're done interviewing potential developers and ready to hire someone, Killips says it is imperative to draft an employment agreement to make sure both parties live up to their end of the bargain.

"That way it is very clear what everyone's obligations are," Killips says. "Who is paying for what, what the rates are going to be, what the milestones are going to be, and what the work product is going to be. It is the best way of ensuring that you get what you pay for."

For Killips, the four most important things to include in any employment or work-for-hire contract are: who is paying whom how much, and when, as well as who is doing what work, and when. He also strongly advises that you restate the nondisclosure agreement should a problem occur and you need to part ways with the programmer.

"If I fire you, that doesn't mean you get to take my idea to the next highest bidder," Killips says. "It doesn't work that way."

Price

Once you receive a signed copy of the agreement, you can move forward in negotiating a potential contract. When it comes to price, freelancers generally charge anywhere from $500 to $7,500 per app, while digital agencies can cost between $10,000 and $500,000. Both freelancers and digital agencies determine how much they charge for each app based on a number of criteria, the most important of which is how complex you want your mobile app to be. Programmers large and small base their pricing on the number of features the app includes. For example, if you want your app to include gaming or social networking elements, you can expect to pay more. Other features that developers charge premium rates for include in-app purchasing, database management, and the ability to use the app on both smartphones and tablets. In the end, the more bells and whistles you want, the more you should expect to pay. In addition, if you used an online service to help you find your freelancer, don't forget about the commission they will collect.

Because the price is going to be based on how you want the app to look and run, this is the time to be as specific as possible with the programmer as you detail your vision for the app. You want the programmer to base their pricing on just how complex you want the app to be. By not being specific, you run the risk of having the freelancer or digital agency come back to you halfway through the project to let you know it is going to cost more than expected. If you carefully detail the different features you are expecting from the app right at the outset, there is a lot less chance for surprises along the way. Because you are protected by your nondisclosure agreement, don't hesitate to lay it all out on the table.

When negotiating a price, it is critical to discuss exactly what you will be getting for your money, not just what features will be included. You want to know how much time they will spend on your app each week, how often they will provide you with status reports, how much debugging and testing they will do, and whether the price includes updating the app after it's been officially released. You want to know that everything you are expecting to be included in the price is, in fact, included, so that there no additional charges arise once the project is under way.

Time

In addition to the cost considerations, you also need to discuss how long the project will take to complete. While ideally you would have your app finished and ready to start selling within a couple of weeks, that's an unlikely scenario in reality. The average time it takes to build a new mobile app from scratch is about three months, but it can often take much longer. Despite your desire to get it built as quickly as possible, you don't want to rush the process. Putting an unrealistic time frame on developers isn't going to get you the results you want. In the end, they will give you a semifinished product that will have little consumer appeal. It won't be user-friendly, it won't look professional, and it definitely won't convince anyone to recommend your app to their friends or buy another app from you in the future.

A good way to keep things on track is to make sure the contract includes certain milestone goals. For example, when the art and interface is done, the programmer will get 25 percent of the fee, and when the gaming functionality is complete, another 25 percent will be paid out. This will help to guarantee that the programmer doesn't try to cram in all the work at the last minute, and will also ensure that you have a chance to review the progress at every step along the way. Because their pay depends on it, these milestone goals are clear incentives for programmers (both freelancers and digital agencies) to stay on schedule.

Regardless of how long you give the developer to finish the app, it will probably take longer than expected. It is hard for programmers to give an accurate time frame for the project before they really get started. The key is accepting that reality up front. Foreseeing delays from the beginning is critical to keeping your frustration in check when deadlines are missed. So while you may agree early on that the developer will turn over a finished mobile app to you in four months, go in with the understanding that it could very well take six or eight months.

Service Draft Agreements

Once you find a freelancer or digital agency with acceptable terms, you can move ahead with drafting a service agreement contract. This will spell out all the details of the job and what's expected, and include the agreed-upon price and project timeline. The contract will also spell out exactly how and when the freelancer or digital agency will be paid (i.e., after certain milestones have been completed). It should include clauses regarding who will own the app when it's finished, terms for termination, and additional confidentiality agreements.

If you are hiring a freelancer, you are responsible for drafting the agreement and getting the person to sign. While a majority of the online freelance job sites do provide their own guarantees and use escrow accounts to ensure that the work is completed as expected before any payments are made to the freelancer, it is still a wise idea to have them sign a "Work for Hire" contract as well. This will provide that extra layer of protection to make sure you are getting what you pay for.

If you are working with a digital agency, you can expect that they will be the ones drafting a work agreement. Be sure to carefully review the contract they provide you with to confirm that all the details—price, timeline, check-in schedule, etc.—are what was agreed upon during your negotiations. Because there are tens of thousands of dollars involved, you would be smart to have a lawyer review the details to make sure there are no hidden surprises. Even if you trust the digital agency completely, contracts often contain details that can be confusing to understand. There is nothing wrong with having an extra set of eyes—especially those of a legal expert—read over the contract. While it might cost you a few hundred dollars up front, it may save you thousands of dollars in the long run in unexpected costs that you didn't know were included in the terms of the contract.

After careful review, if you feel comfortable both with the contract and either the freelancer or digital agency, you can sign your contract to get the programming process officially under way.

Chapter Recap

Here is a recap of the things you need to find out about each freelancer or digital agency you are considering hiring for your programming needs:

1. How much experience do they have programming mobile apps?
It is important to ensure that the person you are going to be working with has the proper experience and skill sets to build an app with the features you want. Get specifics on the platforms they have worked on and the specific types of apps they have built. Make sure everything meshes with your expectations.

2. Can they provide examples of past work?
Have them show you some of the mobile apps they have previously worked on. While you might not care for the type of app, play around with it to see if you like the look, functionality, and interface. If those things aren't your style, look elsewhere.

3. What are past clients saying?

For freelancers, finding this out is easy. Most of the online job-matching sites include options for both rating a programmer's work and detailing the overall status of the working relationship. For digital agencies, looking at online reviews and contacting past clients is a great way to gain insight into what it is like to work with this company. While one bad review shouldn't be a deal-breaker, a handful of them could signal that this person or company isn't worth working with.

4. Will they sign a nondisclosure agreement?

Nondisclosure agreements are legal documents that protect you from having a free-lancer or digital agency steal your idea and market it without you. These are standard legal documents in the mobile app industry, so anyone who refuses to sign one is probably not worth the investment risk.

5. How much will they charge?

It is up to you to describe precisely what your app should look like, how it should function, and the extra features it should have so that your programmer can give you an accurate cost estimate. Not specifying everything you want from the beginning will only result in extra charges along the way.

6. How long will it take?

Don't set unrealistic expectations about how quickly they should be able to finish your app. These things take time, often much longer than anticipated. You don't want to rush the process and end up paying thousands of dollars for an unprofessional and bug-riddled app because you were too eager to start making money.

You may think that once you have successfully hired your freelancer or digital agency, the hard work is over, but that's not the case. In reality, the hardest part of the process—clearly explaining your vision—is just getting under way. While the programmer will have a general idea of the type of app you want and the features you expect it to include, you haven't discussed every last detail.

At this point, the first thing you want to do is sit down and start writing about the app. Get it all down on paper—everything from what the app is and what it will do to how it will look and operate. You want to be as detailed as possible. Think big, like what features it will have and how the interface will function, and think little, such as its colors, fonts, and formatting. Remember, this isn't the programmer's idea; it's yours. It isn't a programmer's job to know what you are thinking; it is his or her job to build what you are thinking. Programmers can't do that if you don't provide detailed descriptions.

In addition to your words, you also want to use drawing and sketches to get your point across. Online, you can find sketching templates that are outline drawings of a mobile device. Print these out for the devices you are developing for and start sketching out what you want each page to look like. Many of the templates also include sections for you to jot down short notes that explain your idea further. You want to do a separate drawing for every page of your app. Don't worry about artistic value; you aren't being judged on that, and the programmer isn't going to take artistic direction from these. The main purpose of these drawings is to supplement your written description so that there is no gap between what you and the programmer are envisioning.

While the vision for the app is yours, you also shouldn't be afraid to listen to your programmer when they throw out suggestions. Because this is your first time developing an app, you're going to find out rather quickly that not every

Expert's View: Working with My Freelancer

Tim Lee

For mobile app developer Tim Lee, drawing was the key to communicating his vision to his programmer for his app, Eat Slow Lose Weight. With his freelancer living in Venezuela, Lee decided to put his limited artistic abilities to good use when trying to convey his vision for the app.

"I don't recommend writing it in words. I drew everything by hand," Lee says. "I don't know how to do art on the computer, so I just took a pen and a piece of paper, and I basically took my iPhone and looked at different apps—I like this part of this app and this part of that app—and I drew what I liked. I drew screens with little stick figures and buttons here and there. I just kept making draft after draft and screen after screen."

When he was finally finished with his sketches, Lee took pictures of each one with his iPhone and sent them directly to his programmer, who was able to review them and ask questions. Lee felt that this provided a clearer picture of his vision, and in turn led to quality discussions between the two about how the app should be built. In the end, he felt the time and effort he put into those drawings paid off in terms of ensuring that his programmer had a full understanding of each aspect of his concept.

Lee said his freelance programmer felt that Lee's style of describing and defining his app was the best and clearest the programmer had come across.

During this stage of the development, Lee says he was talking to his freelancer on Skype for several hours a day to guarantee that they were both on the same page about the app and exactly how it should look and function. One thing Lee advises mobile app developers to consider when hiring a freelancer is time zones. He and his freelancer were on opposite schedules, which put an extra strain on the relationship.

"Mostly when I was asleep, he was awake, and when he was asleep, I was awake, so that was kind of a pain, but I had a good feeling about him, so I put up with it," Lee says. "I would stay up an hour or two later every night to talk to him on Skype, just to hash things out."

Once he had a full picture of what to build, Lee says the conversations between the two slowed while the actual programming was occurring. The two would have weekly conversations about the status of the app and where each aspect—art, interface,

(Continued on next page)

etc.—stood. But even during the slow periods, Lee would push for weekly updates to confirm everything was still on track.

"The conversation [levels] really vary depending on where you are in the process," Lee says.

As for how long the complete programming and testing phases take, Lee suggests throwing all your projections out the window.

"Take any of your estimates and times it by two at least," he says. "This was my first time doing it, so I thought it would take three months—four months, maybe—but the total time took about a year. Eight months to a year seems to be normal, even if you have a simple app. Just know your estimates are always going to be wrong."

idea you have will necessarily be possible. Most likely, you will have chosen to work with someone who has past experience and has some good ideas on how to improve your original vision. Even though your initial instinct might be to say "no," more often than not you will realize that programmers do know what they're talking about, and their ideas can actually be pretty good. You don't want to come off as being overly territorial. The key is making the app as appealing to consumers as possible. So regardless of whose idea it is, as long as it is what's best for the app, you should be in favor of it.

Once you are both on the same page regarding all aspects of how the app will look and function, you can turn the reins over and let them do their work.

Keeping Programmers Focused

It's your job to stay on top of programmers to push them along through the programming and testing stages. Most likely, yours isn't the only app they're working on. So while it is your main priority, it might not be theirs. By holding weekly or twice-weekly check-in meetings, you can keep the pressure on to move forward. Whether it is a freelancer or digital agency, they're not going to want to continually show up for these meetings with nothing new to report.

You should be apprised every time your programmer starts working on a new phase of the app. That gives you a chance to review what has been completed, and it will also serve as an opportunity to remind him or her of the key things the new stage needs to accomplish. It is another chance to make certain you are both seeing things from the same point of view as the project moves forward.

Before you even get started, perhaps even as early as during negotiations, you should be setting regularly scheduled check-ins on the calendar. Because these won't be surprises, the programmer has no excuse for having nothing to report. A definite sign of a problem is when you aren't seeing consistent updates that show the progress being made. If the programmer is giving the same status update several weeks in a row, you absolutely need to push for answers as to why.

Your contract should include milestone goals, so insisting that those are being met isn't too much to ask for. While you go into the programming phase knowing very well that it could take longer than planned, it shouldn't be a matter of programmers dragging their feet or spending more time working for someone else. You are paying them to do a job, and to do it professionally. So when they aren't, it is your responsibility to call them out on it. If you start allowing them to miss deadlines or attend check-in meetings unprepared, their behavior will only get worse.

While you don't want to come off as completely unreasonable or difficult to work with, there is a happy medium that says, "Yes, I am a nice person who may be doing this for the first time, but that doesn't mean I am not a professional, or that I don't deserve the same respect I am giving."

You definitely don't want to wait until the app is finished before playing with it. Even though the app will go through a complete testing phase when the programming is finished, you should still be testing it as it goes along. Because many of the components are connected when building the app, having to go back at the end and redo a section you didn't like could result in their having to reprogram the whole thing.

Each time the programmer sends you a sample, you should test it to make sure it runs as it is supposed to. If you run across something that isn't performing as expected, write down exactly what is happening so that you can share it with your programmer. This would also be a good time to have someone else—friends or family members—play around with it on their devices to see what bugs and errors they discover.

It is important to remember that, when working with computers and mobile technology, not everything is going to work perfectly from the beginning. There isn't a single app that comes through the programming phase completely unscathed and free of problems. While it may be frustrating to receive a half-finished app filled with bugs and mistakes, this is all part of the app development process. Most bugs aren't

Expert's View: Working with Multiple Freelancers

Peter Kruger

New York City's Peter Kruger was getting his MBA from the Tuck School of Business when he decided to develop his first app. Geared toward music lovers, Rock Lobby enables concertgoers to rate live music, write reviews, and upload photos directly from their mobile device.

Because he wanted to have Rock Lobby on both Apple and Android platforms, Kruger says he ended up hiring two different freelancers—one from Portugal, who focused on iOS, and another from the United States, who worked on the Android version—to build his app.

By working with two different programmers from two different countries, Kruger says he saw two very different work styles. While both programmers were professional, he says each one kept him apprised of the status of the app in a different way.

The programmer in Portugal would send Kruger two updates each day: one in the morning, with what he planned to work on, and one in the evening, summarizing what he had done and what goals he was setting for the next day. The programmer also sent a working copy of the app each night, so Kruger was able to test out the work that was done each day. The American programmer was a bit different in that he kept an open Skype chat with Kruger all day long so he could keep up-to-date in real time with what was going on. The constant chatting back and forth made it feel as if the two were working side by side.

"They each had a little bit of a different style, and I matched my management skills to how each preferred to work," Kruger says. "It was easier working with the Portugal freelancer, because it allowed me to focus more of my time on things such as preparing marketing materials and doing the business-related aspects, like expenses."

Kruger says seeing a copy of the app each day was a big help. So, in addition to requesting regular updates on the status of the project, you should also be having the freelancer or digital agency send you test versions of the app throughout the process. If it isn't every day, it should be regularly. While these apps will be rough and far from a polished product, they will give you the opportunity to track the progress that is being made, as well as provide actual feedback for the work that has been completed.

too hard to fix, so the key is simply finding and noticing the mistakes. If you aren't testing throughout each stage of the programming, there is a good chance you will miss something that could in the end either delay your mobile app from hitting the shelves and making money, or cause you to lose out on future customers because your app isn't very user-friendly.

Chapter Recap

While you may be running this business on your own, if you don't have a technical background, it's likely you will be working with someone else during the programming phase of your project. Here are the key things to remember when working with a free-lance programmer or digital agency:

1. You must be as detailed as possible when describing your vision for your app to your programmer. If written words aren't clear enough, try sketching things out.

2. It's okay to take advice from your programmer, who probably has much more experience than you, and can provide some valuable insight into which of your ideas will and will not work.

3. Once the actual programming commences, be sure you are checking in with your programmer regularly to make sure the project is on track.

4. If the programmer shows up for weekly meetings with updates that are always recycled from past weeks, that's a sign there could be a problem.

5. Ask to be apprised each time work gets under way on a new aspect of the app.

6. Review the programmer's progress at each step along the way so that you don't get to the end only to find out that what the person worked on two months ago isn't what you wanted. This will cause major delays.

7. Don't rush the process. You want to keep things on track, but trying to rush the app to market will only result in an app that doesn't get Apple or Google's approval, and will eventually need more work, will not appeal to consumers, and will make very little money.

Testing and Submitting for Approval

Eventually, after months of work—and potentially some poking and prodding on your part—the programmer will be "finished" with the app. While the majority of the heavy lifting may be done, your job as a developer is not yet complete. At this point, you need to put your app through a rigorous testing phase. While your app may never be perfect, it needs to run and operate smoothly enough so that consumers aren't turned off.

Selling an app filled with errors and bugs will only result in lost clientele. After buying an app that doesn't work and is always crashing, it is highly unlikely mobile device users would return to you as customers. Though they may have only spent a dollar or two on the app, they won't be willing to risk the money again on a dud when there are so many other properly working apps from which to choose.

Initial Testing

When the programmer hands the app over, you will serve as the initial tester. It is your job to play around with the app, trying to create different scenarios in which the app stops working properly. Whether it is causing the app to totally crash or freeze, or just finding a certain section that can't be accessed, you want to be the first one to find the errors.

But testing isn't something you can do all on your own. You'll want to find others to help you test out your app. This process of having outsiders test the app is commonly referred to as "beta testing." At first, your group of beta testers will most likely comprise friends, family members, and others you are close to. As time goes on, you will want to expand your group of testers to others in the industry, and other mobile device users who are outside your immediate circle of friends and family. This will help to ensure that you are finding as many of the errors as you can.

Opening up the testing process to others also helps to ensure that the app works on a cross section of devices and operating systems. For example, if you are creating an iOS app, you should test it out to see how it works on all of the devices on which it's built to run, including the iPhone, iPod Touch, or iPad. Additionally, not everyone is constantly updating their operating systems. With that in mind, you want to make sure you have a way to confirm that the app works not only on the most current operating system, but on some older versions as well.

Beta Testing

To do the testing, developers have a number of choices. Both Apple and Google Play, Android's largest app seller, have their own options for beta testing through their developer working environments.

Apple Beta Testing

To start beta testing via Apple, you need to follow several steps to get the app loaded up and all of your testers' mobile devices properly registered.

Once you have a wide range of testers who are using a variety of devices, you need to collect each one's specific device ID. To get each ID number, the device owners can connect their iPhones, iPods, or iPads to iTunes via their computer. Once connected, they click on the "Summary" tab, where specific details about their device will pop up. If they click on the "Serial Number" label, the device ID will appear. These numbers are critical to getting all of your beta testers properly signed up.

After gathering the ID numbers, you can visit the Apple Developer website's "Certificates, Identities & Profiles" section and click on the "Device" tab. To add a device, click on the "Plus" button at the top of the page and select "Register Device." You can then add in the names and IDs of each device, giving your testers access to your unpublished app.

Once your testers are registered, there are a number of other processes that must be completed before they can start using your new app. The additional steps include creating a distribution certificate and ad hoc provisional profile, which can be done via the Apple Developer website, and creating an iOS Apple App Store Package, which can be done through the Xcode software. These give you and your testers the necessary tools to start downloading the app onto each device.

After your beta testers receive the Apple App Store Package you have created, they should install it onto their computers. Once they have done so, they can log in to iTunes and start downloading the app to their device by clicking on the link in the Apps section of the library.

Once the testing begins, the app keeps a record of each time it crashes and sends it back to you every time the device is reconnected to iTunes. Knowing that, it is important to remind your beta testers to regularly connect back to iTunes so you are able to get feedback on a constant basis.

Google Play Beta Testing

Just recently, Google Play released beta testing capabilities for Android apps directly through the Google Play Developer platform. As you do with Apple, you specify certain users who are allowed to download your app via the Google Play Store. To set up beta testing through Google Play, you need to log in to the Google Play Developer Console. Most likely, you already registered the app when testing it out in the building stage. If for some reason you haven't, all you need to do is click on the "Add New Application" link toward the top of the page. Simply give it a name—and it doesn't have to be the official name the app will be sold under—and then download the unpublished application to get the testing process under way.

In addition to testing, this is where you go to finish up other steps of the publication process, including setting up your Google Play Store listing, choosing the countries where you want the app to be sold, setting prices, and allowing for in-app billing if necessary.

Once you have your app downloaded to the Google Play Developer Console, you can start designating who your testers are going to be. This is done by creating a special Google Group or Google+ Community. Once you have set your groups, the Google Play Developer Console will provide you with a unique URL that must be sent to each of your testers. Going to this URL gives each beta tester the chance to read up on what exactly their role entails, and how to opt into the process. After agreeing to the tester terms, they can visit Google Play to download the app and start playing with it.

The Google Play beta testing process is set up to have your testers e-mail you with their feedback on how the app is performing. It is important to make sure you stay on top of your testers to make sure they are actually taking the time to use the various aspects and features, and sending you updates as they do so.

The testing phase only works if the testers are living up to their end of the bargain. As when you're working with your programmers, it is critical to prod your testers along to ensure that you are getting the timely and important feedback you need.

Third-Party Beta Testing: TestFlight

If you would rather not use the Apple and Google beta testing options, there are also third-party testing providers. TestFlight is the outside online service that many developers are turning to first for help in distributing their apps to testers. Originally only available for Apple apps, TestFlight now has Android capabilities and is useful for all developers. The free service is a simple way to send your app to your testers and collect feedback on what they find.

All you need to do to use TestFlight as a developer is register, upload your app to the site, and construct your team of beta testers. Once they're signed up, they can download the app straight to their own devices. It is then their job to do what you had previously attempted: Try to crash the app. They should try to access every feature on the app to see what happens, and make sure nothing they do makes the app stop functioning.

Once your beta testers start using the app, TestFlight gives you access to metrics that show how and what testers are doing when using the app on their device. This allows you to see in real time exactly what is happening with the app, freeing you from having to wait for each tester to report back on his or her progress. Instead of receiving a report from your testers on what they were doing when the app crashed, you are immediately alerted via TestFlight about the problem and what the tester was doing when it happened. With this method, you aren't as dependent on timely feedback from your testers.

Other features of TestFlight include the ability to set checkpoints on the app to see which sections the testers are reaching, and which aspects are the most popular. It also lets you trigger in-app questions for your testers that they can answer as they visit various sections.

Other Third-Party Beta Testing Services

In addition to TestFlight and other popular online beta testing services, like UserTesting, there are also online services for developers who are having a hard time coming up with an effective beta testing group. While not free, these services give you the ability to test your app on a much wider cross section of users. These services boast the power to match you with testers of all ages, genders, and backgrounds. Among

some of the more popular beta testing matching services are Elusive Stars (www
.elusivestars.com), The Beta Family (http://thebetafamily.com), and iBetaTest (http://
ibetatest.com).

Freelancers or digital agencies may say that they can handle the testing in-house
without a group of outside beta testers. While many times they do extensive testing
that results in a fully functioning and error-free app, it doesn't hurt to conduct your
own testing. Even if it is just you and a handful of family and friends who end up
reviewing it, having an extra set of trusted eyes on it can't hurt.

Because your contract may stipulate that your programmer's work on the app
is totally finished once it starts being sold, you want to have additional testers that
you trust check it out to make sure the freelancer or digital agency isn't rushing it to
market just so they can collect their check.

Eventually you will reach a point where your beta testers are no longer running
into problems and you think you're ready to move forward. The next step is seeing if
Apple and Google agree.

Expert's View: The Three Phases of App Testing

Joshua Weiss

In the three years that Joshua Weiss has been creating mobile apps, he has developed
an extensive testing phase designed to make sure the app is always performing up
to expectations. Weiss, who helped to cofound his mobile application development
company, TeliApp, says he uses a three-part testing phase that includes him and other
members of his company, those they work with on the research and marketing phases
of the project, and the app users themselves.

"It is rigorous, it is hard, and it is not to be taken lightly," Weiss says of TeliApp's testing.

Alpha Testing

The first stage, which Weiss refers to as "alpha testing," involves having only TeliApp
employees play around with the app. While this originally was just Weiss, the company
has grown, and he's now able to get all twelve members of TeliApp involved in the process. He says the main goal during this stage is for everyone to try everything they can
to get the app to stop functioning.

"Alpha testing is when you are done programming the app but haven't really tested it much," Weiss says. "It involves, generally, employees of the company using the app as actively as possible, and either trying to crash the server or just crash the app itself. We want them to see if they can create scenarios and circumstances that will cause the app to crash and act buggy."

When employees are able to find ways to get the app to stop operating properly, they fill out an incident report and explain to the programmers how they were able to crash the application.

"They then attempt to replicate it, and they will say, 'Aha, I missed a line of code here, or this line should have looked like this, or I forgot to account for that.' They will go ahead and fix it and then develop a new one and publish it internally," Weiss says. "Then we will go ahead and test that one."

The key, Weiss says, is always making sure every person testing the app is always using the most current version. Each time a problem is identified and then solved, Weiss has his team delete the app and start fresh with the newest version.

Beta Testing

After a substantial amount of time kicking the tires in-house, Weiss says the testing stage shifts to what they refer to as "beta testing." This involves letting others outside his immediate development team see the app for the first time.

"Beta testing involves publishing it to a slightly broader audience," Weiss says. "These are not employees of the company, but people that we work with when we are asking research and marketing questions. We will give them access to the same app and ask them to use it actively and see if they can crash it."

Similar to what is done during their initial testing stage, each time testers are able to get the app to stop working properly, they take note of it and let the programmers know so they can immediately start working on a solution.

While these stages serve as a great way to find those initial bugs, they can't answer all the company's questions, Weiss says. In particular, these testing stages aren't able to show you what happens when a large number of people, say, in the thousands, access your app at the same time. A group of thirty or forty testers isn't going to put the pressure on the network that developers are sometimes looking for.

(Continued on next page)

"The problem with certain apps is that you need a much larger audience to test the true functionality," he says. "So sometimes a company is forced to publish an app and use the first couple of months as the beta test itself. I don't see any way around this, because you can't give it to five thousand people."

Gamma Testing

The final stage is what Weiss and his team call "gamma testing." This is the ongoing support and testing that they give their apps after they hit the market. Weiss stresses that even though you might have conducted extremely detailed alpha and beta testing, you must ensure that your app is bug-free even after consumers start buying it.

"This is just keeping up with the times," Weiss says of the gamma testing phase. "You are constantly using your users and kind of pretending that you are always testing. It is not like the app is done and now we publish it and good luck to you. There is constant interaction, because there is no way to account for every mistake. There will be circumstances and scenarios that will be created that you will never have thought of. New devices, different configurations, different circumstances, different apps that might interact or behave differently on the person's phone that are unique to that person's circumstances. There are all of these different scenarios that you can't account for."

Weiss believes the thorough testing contributes to his apps' success.

Apple Approval

Now that the app is bug-free and ready for the public, you still can't just send it to the Apple App Store or Google Play Store and watch the money start rolling in. Apple, Google, Amazon, and the other Android marketplaces get a chance to review the app to make sure it meets their standards. Generally speaking, Apple's benchmarks for approval are much more stringent than those required by the Android stores.

Mobile app developer Josh Weiss says that one of the most important factors in deciding whether or not to submit an app for approval is whether it has any bugs that will cause Apple, Google, or any of the other Android marketplaces to reject it.

Google, Weiss says, takes a very passive approach when deciding whether or not to publish an app, essentially taking developers at their word that the apps do exactly what is described. It only stops an app from being sold if it receives user complaints that the app isn't functioning as it should. Apple takes a much more rigorous approach, according to Weiss.

"They go through every line of code to make sure your app does what it says it can, and that you don't use procedures and methods for one thing that are intended for another," Weiss says. "There is a whole rulebook that developers must understand and read thoroughly when they develop for Apple. If you deviate from those rules, in all likelihood your app will not be published."

If you are developing your app for the iOS platform and are ready to submit it to Apple, you need to know they are going to be reviewing it with a fine-toothed comb. From checking functionality, security, and privacy to making sure it doesn't contain violent, pornographic, or otherwise objectionable content, Apple conducts a thorough analysis to make sure the app is ready for sale. Overall, Apple uses a more than one hundred–point checklist to review every app submitted to the store. Part of Apple's appeal is how well its apps operate. The company isn't going to risk its reputation on you or your app if it isn't 100 percent sure it lives up to their expectations.

Apple is very up-front during this process. Simply put, if the app doesn't meet the company's high standards, it's not getting approved and not going to be sold in the app store. It is not uncommon for developers to see their apps initially rejected by Apple. This doesn't mean those apps can never be sold; what it means is that those developers will have to fix the problems Apple has noted. If it is a content problem, that's on you to resolve. If it is a technical issue, it's up to your programmer—whether that's you, a freelancer, or a digital agency—to try and fix the bugs.

Apple Appeals

The good news is that Apple typically reviews and rules on apps within a week, so you'll find out rather quickly if it is good to go or still needs more work. If you feel your app has been rejected unfairly, you can file an appeal with the Apple app-review board to try to get the rejection overturned. You can file your appeal by logging in to the Apple Developer website and clicking on the "Contact" link near the bottom of the page. Once on the contact page, click the "Appealing an App Rejection" link under the Apple App Store section to start filling out the appeal form.

The form gives you the opportunity to explain why you think the app was rejected in error and why the issues the team has with the app are unfounded. It is important to remember that the likelihood of an appeal being overturned for content reasons is slim. If Apple finds that your app has no entertainment value or is offensive, your explanation probably won't do much good. However, if the issues are technical, there have been many instances of developers successfully clarifying why they coded the way they did. Be forewarned, however: The appeals process can take several weeks. It may just be easier to try to fix the problems that Apple has pointed out and resubmit the app for approval.

Once you do get Apple's official blessing on your app, you can either send it to the Apple App Store to immediately begin sales, or schedule a future release date. Because you will be doing marketing—and lots of it—to help the app build some consumer demand, scheduling a future date allows you time to lay out that marketing plan. However, if you are eager to start seeing the money come in, you do have the option of immediately selling the app.

Google Play and Android Approval

If you are developing Android apps—whether exclusively, or in addition to iOS apps—you will need to get them approved by Google, Amazon, or the other Android marketplaces. This process is considerably less stringent than the detailed grilling that Apple conducts.

Instead of checking your app's code line by line to ensure that it operates as advertised, Google pays more attention to the content to confirm it isn't offensive. Specifically, the content can't be considered sexually explicit, violent, or a form of bullying, and it also cannot contain any type of hate speech directed toward a specific race, ethnicity, religion, disability, gender, age, veteran status, or sexual orientation.

Google also makes sure the app is not misrepresenting itself by claiming to be affiliated with another person, business, or other type of organization when it is not, or stealing another app's intellectual property. Additionally, Google double-checks the app to make sure it isn't stealing a user's personal information or passing them spam, viruses, Trojans, or other types of malware that can infect a smartphone or tablet.

One of the final aspects of Google's app check is whether or not the app you submitted sucks up a user's network capability. Google policy states that the app cannot create erratic network usage that negatively affects the mobile device's service charges.

Unlike the Apple approval process, which can be somewhat unpredictable at times, if your app is straightforward and not offensive to others, there is a good chance it will be published. And unlike Apple, which averages about five days to approve or reject an app, Google makes its determination within hours. This means there is no reason to submit for approval and then schedule a release date at a later time because the app can start being downloaded on the same day you submit. With Android, just be sure to have all your ducks in a row before your submit for approval, because shortly after you do, it will be live for everyone to see and buy.

With Google, the best approach is to finish beta testing and wrap up all your Google Play in-store promotional materials. That means selecting graphics, screenshots, and product descriptions that you want featured on your Google Play product page. The product page is what mobile device owners will see when deciding whether or not to purchase the app.

While we delve into this more in the marketing and promotions section of the book, chapters 11 and 12, the product page needs to include an enticing description that will intrigue smartphone and tablet owners enough to risk the money on your app. It is important to have more than just a solid description. All good product pages have screenshots showing off the best of what the app has to offer.

Many developers are also turning to video to help sell their apps. Specifically, videos show demonstrations of exactly how the app is used or played. This helps take the guesswork out of determining what an app might actually be like. Seeing it in action helps free mobile device owners of any fears that they won't like the app after they buy it.

If you plan to sell your app in multiple countries, Google gives you the option of localizing a product page for each nation. This allows you the opportunity to localize your product page to target people of different backgrounds and cultures.

Once you have your product page completed, you can simply pick the day you want the app to be released. Because it only takes a few hours for the app to be checked out by Google, submitting the app for approval in the morning means it should be published and ready to be downloaded by smartphone and tablet users by mid-afternoon.

Google Play Appeals

If for some reason your app is rejected by Google, you do have the ability to make the suggested corrections and resubmit. However, too many rejected apps will land you on the outside of the Google Play Store. Multiple policy violations can result in your developer account being terminated. If you feel the mistakes that are being pointed out are being misconstrued somehow, you do have the ability to appeal Google's decision.

To appeal, you need to fill out an appeals contact form through the Google Play Developer Console at https://support.google.com/googleplay/android-developer/contact/appappeals. You need to disclose on the form why your app was rejected, and then explain why it shouldn't have been. You only have five hundred words to make your case, so be brief and get to your point. If Google has rejected your app because they think you have stolen intellectual property from someone else and used it for yourself, you have the option to attach any necessary documents that prove you hold the rights to that property. Once you have completed the form, click "Submit" and wait for Google to send you a response via e-mail.

If Google rules in your favor, the app will be reinstated. If Google rules against you, the decision is final, and your only options are to fix the mistakes or sell your app in one of the other Android marketplaces.

Amazon Approval

If you want to sell your app in the Amazon Appstore—allowing Kindle users to have access to it—you will need to go through a completely separate approval process. Amazon's approval process is considered more in line with Apple's, in that the company gives every app a thorough testing to make sure it meets high standards. Rather than looking at design or any aspect of innovation, the Amazon testing process is done as a way to confirm that the app works as spelled out in the product description, doesn't damage the mobile device in any way, and isn't putting any data at risk. Similar to Google Play, Amazon also checks for content issues to make sure the app isn't offensive or contain intellectual property that are the rights of someone else.

While the length of time varies for each person, Amazon approval time tends to run between two and three weeks. You are kept abreast of how the approval process is coming along in your Amazon Mobile App Distribution Portal, as well as via e-mail. When Amazon has finished testing the app, they will send you an e-mail informing you whether the app has been approved or rejected. If it has been rejected, they will also provide you with details on why the app failed the test, and what can be done to make it conform to their guidelines.

Amazon Appeals

Unlike Apple and Google, which give you a chance to appeal a rejected app, Amazon gives users the opportunity to make changes before it ever gets to that point. After submitting your app for approval, you can keep track of its status in your Amazon Mobile App Distribution Portal. At some point, the app will either be approved, placed in the store, or marked as pending, which means it needs your further attention. At this point, Amazon will send you an e-mail highlighting exactly what must be addressed in order for the app to be formally approved. If those changes are never made, Amazon will eventually reject the app, forcing you to start the whole process over.

■ ■ ■

Whether you're developing for Apple, Google, Amazon, or any of the other marketplaces, you need to take the testing stage extremely seriously. Your goal isn't just to have the app slip through the approval process; you want to pass with flying colors. You want your app to be as functionally sound as possible, because that could mean the difference between your business really taking off or sinking after your first app. A polished-looking app that performs as advertised gives you the chance to earn repeat customers. Apps with bugs, even just one, aren't going to lure consumers into buying a second one from you.

Your goal isn't just to get mobile device users to download your app; your goal is to ensure that they are so impressed with what you have developed that they would buy others from you. Building a successful business requires building a dedicated consumer base, and that can only be done by developing an app that not only lives up to, but exceeds, all expectations.

Chapter Recap

The testing process is one of the most critical stages of development. You only have one chance to make a great impression on would-be customers, so giving them an app that functions as promised is key. The only way to make that happen is to subject your app to a rigorous testing phase. Here are the key things to remember when testing your app and submitting it for approval:

- When your app is finished being programmed, either by yourself or by the outside programmer you hired, it still needs a considerable amount of testing before it can be submitted for approval.

- In addition to your own testing, it is important to put together a group of testers not involved in the app's development—beta testers—to check it over from top to bottom.

- In addition to the Apple and Google options, you can use third-party services, such as the popular TestFlight, to conduct the beta testing phase.

- The approval process varies by marketplace. If you are developing for Apple or Amazon, be prepared for a very thorough testing stage that could result in numerous rejections for one reason or another. If you plan on only selling your app in the Google Play Store, expect a much more lenient process.

- Getting your app approved can take anywhere from a few hours with Google to a few days with Apple and a few weeks with Amazon.

- If your app is rejected for one reason or another, your options are to make the necessary changes and resubmit for approval; decide the app isn't worth fixing, and start over from scratch; or appeal the ruling.

10 Selling Your App

The goal of any business is to be profitable, so the next step in building your venture is determining how you're going to make money off your app. Should you charge 99 cents and ask users to pay to download it, or should you make it free and use other tactics to monetize the app? This can be one of the most difficult questions for an app developer to answer. While you can always change your pricing strategy, getting it wrong at the beginning means you could risk losing out on a number of potential customers.

You have three main choices for monetizing your app: charging for downloads, in-app purchasing, and in-app advertising. While all three options have the ability to make you money, they each have some pros and cons, so it is important to evaluate each one in order to accurately determine which fits your app best. It is important to remember that whichever option you choose, Apple, Google, and Amazon each take 30 percent of all app revenue, regardless of which setup the money comes from.

Download Purchases

The simplest way to monetize your app is to charge mobile device users to download. This is when you designate your app for the paid sections of the Apple, Google, and Amazon app stores and charge users a set price up front for the app. To download the app to their devices, smartphone and tablet owners must first pay for the app. In the different app stores, these apps are the ones designated as "paid" apps. There is no restriction on how much you can charge for the app, although if you price it too high—typically, more than $1.99—you probably won't find too many consumers willing to shell out the extra cash.

Once smartphone or tablet owners pay for the download, they aren't charged anything further to use the app or any of its features. Paying up front gives the users full access to the app, without the need to spend any more money. Mobile device users tend to like this option, because they pay a small fee at the beginning, usually 99 cents or $1.99, and aren't asked for any more money after that. It is a one-time fee that frees them of any future monetary demands. This means that any time you update the app, everyone who has already paid to download it gets the new version for free.

From the developer's perspective, this is the simplest way to make money, because you set the price and collect your money each time a download occurs. With the other options, you are dependent upon the user liking the app and being willing to spend more to use additional features.

There are several drawbacks to choosing this method, however. First, many mobile device users refuse to pay for an app regardless of how cheap it may be. So by choosing to charge to download your app, you are turning off a sizable number of potential users. Because you want to attract as many users as possible, this alone is a reason that many developers choose to go in another monetizing direction.

Another disadvantage to this method is that there is no way to charge users anything extra should you upgrade the app or add a cool new feature. So while the new feature may help you attract new customers, it won't help you profit off the consumers you already have. The only way to make more money off those original downloaders is to build another app that entices them to download again.

In-App Purchases

The monetizing option becoming most popular to developers recently has been in-app purchases. In-app purchases can be used either in tandem with a paid app or with apps that are free to download. For app users, these purchases are made while using the app itself. When users try to access a feature or function that has to be paid for, they are notified and asked if they want to spend the money. To make an in-app purchase, mobile device owners are required to provide their app store password as confirmation that they understand they are being charged for these features.

In-app purchases give you the ability to charge mobile device users extra money to gain additional features or functions of the app. With games, this might mean that for an extra charge—the in-app purchase—the user can play different levels not available to those who only downloaded the app itself. With a news app, this might mean a monthly subscription for daily content. This is a way to give smartphone or tablet owners a small taste of the app first, with an eye toward enticing them to pay more for additional content later.

Regardless of the store in which you plan to sell the app, in-app purchasing can only be used to sell virtual goods or services, and cannot be used to sell any type of real-world items. For example, a developer who also works as an insurance agent can't build an app and include an in-app purchasing option to buy car insurance. Whatever is being sold on the app must be a virtual item.

Apple currently lets developers offer four different types of in-app purchases:

- Non-replenishable: These are in-app purchases that only need to be bought once. They can also be transferred to multiple devices under the same iTunes account.
- Replenishable: These in-app purchases are only good for one use, such as extra lives in a game.
- Subscriptions: These in-app purchases give users access to certain features or digital content in the app for a set time frame (e.g., a month or year). Once that expires, users need to use the in-app purchase again to continue their subscription.
- Auto-renewing subscriptions: These in-app purchases are just like subscriptions, and are automatically renewed unless the user specifies otherwise.

Google, on the other hand, breaks down its in-app purchases into two categories: one-time billing, where users are only charged once for the in-app purchase they buy, and recurring billing, which is used for subscriptions that need to be renewed regularly. Similar to Google Play's offering, Amazon gives mobile app developers the opportunity to use in-app purchasing. However, the technology used to do so is different for each app store, so it is important to understand the exact specifications each requires when programming the app to ensure that it meets all requirements for app store approval.

In-app purchasing has become popular with developers in recent years because it's making them the most money. Recent research has found that apps that utilize in-app billing generate more revenue than both paid apps and free apps that are supported with ads. Specifically, the study by the app store analytics firm Distimo revealed that Apple apps with in-app purchases make an average of 20 cents more per app download. Overall, in-app purchasing is accounting for roughly three-quarters of all the revenue generated in the Apple App Store.

In addition to its ability to generate revenue, another benefit of the in-app purchase monetary strategy is that it allows developers to give consumers a taste of their app without having to program a separate free or "lite" version.

If you are programming the app yourself, it will essentially take nearly twice as long to program both a full and a free version, and if you are paying someone else to do it, expect nearly double the cost. Building one app that essentially locks off certain parts to users who aren't willing to pay for it is a way to save time and money during the programming stage.

In-app purchasing also is a way to make more money off users when the app is updated. Instead of including the updated features in the free portion of the app, create a new section for the updated features that can only be accessed through an in-app purchase. Instead of the paid download option, where you can only make money off the downloader once, the in-app purchasing business model allows you regular opportunities to generate revenue off the same app from the same customer.

There are a few drawbacks to using the in-app purchasing method, however. If you have taken the route of letting users download the app initially for free, you now have the extra task of enticing them to spend money on it. This can be tough, because some users just refuse to pay for an app. They are completely averse to that idea, no matter what is offered in return. So while they might be willing to download your app for free, there isn't anything you can do to convince them that spending money on an in-app purchase is a wise investment.

Research shows that developers can expect only about a 5 percent conversion rate on in-app purchases. This means that for every one hundred smartphone and tablet owners that download the app for free, just five will end up spending money on an in-app purchase. So while this model can be more lucrative than the others, it only works if you are able to garner a large audience. Because the conversion rate is so small, there is extra pressure to develop an app that has wide appeal. If it doesn't, your chances of the app becoming profitable are quite slim.

Another drawback to in-app purchasing is that many devices offer the option of turning in-app purchasing off. While this is done mainly by parents wanting to make sure their kids aren't wasting money, it does mean that some of your consumers won't even have the option of paying for any additional content or features. Though this isn't a large number, it is just another aspect to consider when choosing a pricing model.

The in-app purchasing strategy is only profitable if you are able to get consumers to continually make regular purchases. If your app doesn't lend itself to this style, you are better served going in one of the other directions.

In-App Advertising

The third option you have to make money off your app is to use in-app advertising. Whether it is a banner or pop-up ad, there are a number of ways developers can feature advertisements in their app in return for payment from the advertiser. While it isn't difficult to find advertisers looking to promote their business on your app, it is a chore to really turn a profit with this method.

To use in-app advertising, you need to find an online ad network service that will match you up with advertisers. These ad networks provide you with the ads and the needed tools to place them in your app. The services generally offer a variety of types of mobile ads, including:

- Banner ads: This is one of the more common types of ads, usually promoted at the top or bottom of the app.
- Interstitial ads: These are full-screen ads that pop up on top of your app's content or while the app is loading. Often, these include video ads.
- Ad prompts: These ads appear in the middle of the screen, similar to how users are prompted to pay for in-app purchases, and ask the user to click to see the entire ad.
- Expanding ad: These ads may start out looking like a banner at the top or bottom of the screen, but they expand to display a larger ad.

The ways to make money through this method vary. After installing the ads on your app via the service, the ad network will pay you when the app is downloaded and actually opened by the user; when the ad in your app is actually clicked on by the mobile device owner; or depending on how many times it is displayed, which is commonly referred to as the number of ad impressions. Each service is different in exactly how it sets up its payment structure, so if you decide to use in-app advertising, it is important to compare each service before choosing one.

The success or failure of in-app advertising really depends on how engaging your app actually is. To make money off in-app advertising, you need the user to click on the in-app ad and continually visit the app to boost the number of ad impressions.

If your app isn't intriguing enough to get mobile device owners to keep using it, this model isn't going to pay off for you. If, however, your app is something that can generate constant repeat users, there is no telling how much money your app can make. The profit potential with this option is huge, but it hinges on whether the app is something users are truly going to connect with.

A significant downside to in-app advertisements is that consumers often find them distracting and annoying. When this is the case, your app needs to be a real star to keep users engaged. If the ads are too distracting, many users will close down the app and never return. Not only will you likely lose out on having that customer's repeat business should you someday build a second app, but you are also losing out on those valuable impressions that many ad services base their payment rates on.

Online Resources: Ad Network Services

If you are going to use the in-app advertising business model, you need to sign up with an ad network service that will connect you with advertisers. In exchange for placing the ads in your app, these services pay you a nominal fee—usually a few cents—each time a mobile device user downloads and opens the app or clicks on the ad from your app. Some of these services include:

- AdMob—www.google.com.my/ads/admob
- iAd—http://advertising.apple.com
- LeadBolt—www.leadbolt.com
- mMedia—http://mmedia.com
- MobFox—www.mobfox.com
- mobhero—www.mobhero.com
- Mojiva—www.mojiva.com
- SendDroid—http://senddroid.com
- Tapjoy—www.tapjoy.com
- ValueClick Media—www.valueclickmedia.com

Also, you want to ensure that the ads don't diminish the app's functionality in any way. If an ad is causing an app to constantly crash or not allowing the user to access certain features, consumers are going to quickly stop using the app—preventing you from a future customer, as well as the ad impressions and clicks that you need to make money.

Unfortunately, another negative to working with ad networks is that they aren't all on the up and up. Some of these networks have been known to use their ads as a way to collect certain personal information from the smartphone and tablet owners using the app in which the ad was placed. This information is often collected without any permission given from the mobile device owner, and is always seen as an invasion of their privacy.

Besides collecting personal information, some ad networks also use their ads to spread viruses and other malware that can also be used to steal personal data and hurt the functionality of the mobile device. Knowing that these services exist makes it even more vital that you do some serious investigating before signing on with an in-app advertising network.

I would highly suggest not only comparing the types of ads and payment structures each ad network offers, but also talking to some of their developers to see how happy they've been with the service. Have the ads been too intrusive or damaging to the apps' performance? Have consumers been complaining to them that their device isn't functioning properly after using the app? Are you making any money this way? These are the types of questions you want to be asking the developers about the ad networks they have used.

This is also an opportunity to look at some of the apps you enjoy using that include in-app advertising. See what types of ads those are, and how they might be incorporated into your app. For the apps that have ads that seem to be a good fit, reach out to those developers to see which ad network they have partnered with.

You don't want to take any shortcuts with your research on these ad networks. Remember, your whole monetization strategy is based on finding the right ad network that is going to not only provide you with a product that is appealing to your consumers, but also a payment structure that is going to make you some money.

If you don't think your app will work well with ads, or that the app isn't going to get the type of sustained use that is needed to profit from in-app advertising, then you really should consider either just charging for your app at the time of the download, or figuring out a way to include in-app purchasing.

■ ■ ■

While all three monetization options have the ability to make money on their own, many developers choose to combine two or three of them to increase their chances of turning a profit. You don't have to pick just one of the three. Many developers have been known to include in-app ads or in-app purchasing on a paid app, or to feature both in-app advertising and in-app purchases on a free app. However, while this does increase your chances of making money, you also run the risk of alienating consumers who may feel you are trying to take advantage of them with your pricing structure.

If this is your first app, and you aren't sure how it will be received by mobile device owners, it is probably best to choose just one of three monetization methods.

Setting a Price

If you have decided to charge users for your app, either via a paid download, in-app purchasing, or a combination of the two, then you need to decide how much to charge. Most first-time developers agree that this process tends to be a trial by fire. Luckily, you aren't bound by any decisions you make. As the app's developer, you always have the option of raising or lowering the prices you originally set.

A good first step is to consider what it is going to take for you to make money off this app. To do this, you need to factor in how much you spent developing the app, as well as how much you plan to spend marketing it.

Start with the programming costs first. If you did all the work on your own, your development costs are probably small, so it won't take as many app downloads or in-app purchases to make money. But if you hired an outside developer (either a freelancer or a digital agency) to build your app, you are going to have to make a lot more money to recoup your costs.

Let's say you spend $2,000 to hire a freelancer to build your app, and decide you want to use the "paid download" monetizing strategy. If you price the app at 99 cents—of which Apple, Google, and Amazon will take 30 percent—it will take you 2,857 downloads just to break even. And that isn't even taking into account how much you spend on marketing. If you end up spending at least another $1,000 on marketing, then it will take you more than 4,200 downloads to break even.

99-Cent Paid Download

Total expenses / developer income
(price per download – app store cut) = break-even point

$3,000 / 69.3 (.99 – 30%) = $2,857

The higher you price your app, of course, the fewer downloads you will need to make your money. If you were to bump the price to $1.99 and keep the same budget for developing and marketing the app, you would need to sell more than 2,100 downloads to break even, or less than 1,500 if you are charging $2.99.

$1.99 Paid Download

$3,000 / 1.39 (1.99 – 30%) = $2,158.20

$2.99 Paid Download

$3,000 / 2.093 (2.99 – 30%) = $1,433.30

If you are using in-app purchasing, in-app advertising methods, or a combination of the two, you need to calculate what your break-even points are for those monetization strategies. For in-app purchases, estimate how many of those purchases you need users to make in order to make some money. Remember that one user can make multiple in-app purchases, so you won't necessarily need as many mobile device owners to download the app in order to break even.

Let's use the example from above, where you spent $2,000 on the development and $1,000 on marketing, but this time you're allowing users to download the app for free, charging them 99 cents for each in-app purchase. To break even you would need to sell 2,857 in-app purchases. But unlike the previous example, you don't need 2,857 different users to reach that number. If each user makes three in-app purchases, it will take significantly fewer downloads to reach your goal.

99-Cent In-App Purchase

$3,000 / 69.3 (.99 – 30%) = $2,857

If you are using strictly in-app advertising, you need to determine how many impressions you will need to make a profit. This will be different for each ad network you work with because each one has a different pricing structure. For example, if the ad network you are working with pays $1.10 per 1,000 ad impressions, then you would need nearly 3.9 million impressions to break even on development and marketing costs of $3,000. Remember, though, that one impression is counted each time the ad is displayed. If a mobile device user opens your app five times a day, that's 1,825 times each year per user. At that rate, you would need 2,137 users to download your app to break even.

$1.10 per 1,000 Ad Impressions

$3,000 / ($1.10 − 30%) = 3,896 x 1,000 = 3.89 million

While doing all of these calculations won't necessarily help you to turn a profit, it is critical to know what will be needed to do so, and these calculations can help you figure that out.

Of course, you'll also want to research the competition to ensure that your prices aren't too far out of whack—no matter what your calculations tell you.

While there might not be another app that does exactly what yours can, there are undoubtedly some that are quite similar. You want to see what developers are charging for those to give yourself an idea of the ballpark you should be in. Seeing how competitors have priced their apps gives you the opportunity to either price cheaper than theirs to try and draw interest; charge the same, and see which ones consumers prefer; or, if you think your app has a lot more to offer, then you can price yours a little higher.

Once you know your break-even point and what the market is paying for something similar, you can set an initial price. Remember, none of these prices—either for paid downloads or in-app purchases—are set in stone. So, don't feel an overwhelming amount of pressure to get the price right from the start; go into this process knowing that it may take some tinkering to find the price that is going to do the best job of enticing mobile device owners to download your app.

Expert's View: App Pricing

Joshua Weiss

New York–based developer Josh Weiss, who has been creating mobile apps since 2010, says his preference is to always use in-app purchasing as a monetization strategy. He says with any new app, unless there is a significant marketing effort—which requires substantial capital—a developer wants to make it as easy as possible for the potential user to make the decision to download the app.

"If you have significant download momentum and can sustain a slight loss of downloads by charging a download fee for your app, that's okay," Weiss says. "But for the new app developer, it is much easier to gain a more significant audience simply by enabling potential users to download the app for free."

Weiss says that when developers give away the app for free, their best monetization option is to create an in-app purchasing opportunity for the user. The challenge with this method is coming up with something the user feels is worthwhile to purchase.

"Now that the user has your app and you've included, hopefully, an in-app purchasing opportunity that the user will need and/or want more than once, you've created a long-term revenue-generating business model," Weiss says, adding that the strategy is much better than relying on the one-time purchase that may never happen.

Weiss is currently in the process of trying to convert his most recent mobile app, Love Struck—which utilizes a proprietary blend of tones that trigger the portions of the brain associated with love and attraction—from a paid download monetization strategy to an in-app purchasing model.

"With no marketing, we had under a dozen downloads of our ninety-nine-cent app," Weiss says. "When we switched the app to free, even with absolutely no marketing, we started getting hundreds of downloads a month. The challenge to us, of course, was to create an in-app purchasing opportunity that is worthwhile to the user."

Weiss says he is currently working on in-app purchasing options and hopes to unveil them soon to see if the switch bolsters sales.

However, not all apps are suited for in-app purchasing. Weiss's iBox Remote File Access app, which enables iOS and Android mobile devices to connect wirelessly to any Windows computer, is an example of an app in which in-app purchasing would be

(Continued on next page)

ineffective. In cases like this, Weiss believes it is critical to find the least-offensive price point for consumers.

"We ask what is the least amount of money that we can ask for this app that will not offend people," Weiss says. "The iBox app is probably worth at least five bucks. You are doing something that is very difficult to do, and doing it very uniquely and smoothly. But we don't charge five bucks; we charge a buck, because we want most people, most of the time, to download it. We don't want to give people a reason to say 'Eh, that's a little too much money for this.' "

That's why one of Weiss's strategies is to go one step further for Android owners. With Android owners much less willing to pay for a mobile app, Weiss says they give iBox away for free in the Google Play Store, while still charging 99 cents for the iOS version.

"We understand that Android has its own culture, and so does iOS. They are different types of people. People that use iOS devices don't mind paying a buck or two for a really good app, but Android users really do care about spending even a dollar on an app. It could be the greatest game in the world, but if it costs a buck, they won't buy it."

Pricing Paid Downloads

While you have the option to price your app as high as you like—well, as high as the preset limits of $1,000 for iOS apps and $200 for Android apps in the Google Play Store—you have to be both realistic and strategic when picking your price. While ideally you would price your app based solely on your break-even point, it is important to remember what your competitors are charging.

Based on the current market, the majority of developers are typically going with one of two choices for their app's price point—99 cents or $1.99. That isn't to say others aren't charging more, because they are, or that you can't charge more, because you can.

If you think your game app is the next in-demand form of entertainment that every teen in the country will be clamoring for, or a business app that no employee can work without, price higher. Or, if your competitors are all charging more, join that crowd. However, be aware that if your app doesn't fulfill a special need in a way that other apps do not, the higher price will be an immediate turnoff for the majority of mobile device owners.

Many app developers agree that mobile device owners won't think twice about spending 99 cents or $1.99 on an app, but when they are asked to spend any more—even if it is just a dollar or two—their wallets usually tighten up.

Yet New York developer Alex Genadinik actually had a lot of success pricing his four business apps at a higher price—at least until a competitor came along and forced him into slashing prices. Genadinik's apps serve as a four-part course on starting a business, complete with tips on coming up with an idea, planning it out, obtaining funding, and marketing suggestions that he felt were worth far more than your typical 99-cent app.

When determining his price, Genadinik says he considered three factors: who his target market was and how affluent they were; how much value the apps provided; and what his competitors were charging for similar apps.

"Pricing in the app stores is very tricky," he says. "I tried a lot of permutations of pricing my app, from ninety-nine cents to ten dollars. I do feel like when people get the most out of my app, they get more than a ten-dollar value for sure. But that isn't the only factor; it's also a matter of convincing them they will get that value beforehand."

For a while, Genadinik says he was doing just that, convincing numerous mobile device owners that his apps were worth the $10 he was charging.

"One of my apps was selling well for ten dollars," Genadinik says. "No one ever complained about the price. But then I had a competitor who created an app right after me and priced it for free. He jumped over me in the rankings and I lost visibility, and that made it difficult [to get new customers]."

To try to reclaim his high visibility in the business app in-store rankings, Genadinik says he was forced to lower his price considerably, to $2. In the end, he says his competitor's decision to give away his app for free ended up being a lose-lose proposition for both of them.

"That ruined things," he says. "That guy isn't making money, and I am making less money. There are some developers like that who participate in this pricing race to the bottom, but no one wins from that. When you pick a price, you have to be flexible with it based on the current environment. Like, if that guy wasn't there, I could still be charging ten bucks, but now that he is there, I have to charge less."

As a first-time developer who wasn't exactly sure what her best price point would be, Caroline Fielding says she worked closely with the digital agency that programmed her Bus Rage app in determining the price.

While the agency originally suggested a higher $2.99 price, Fielding says she felt more comfortable at $1.99, and started it off there. However, after a month of rather tepid sales and some feedback from family and friends, she decided to lower the price.

"It just wasn't going so well, so I dropped it myself, to ninety-nine cents," Fielding says. "I thought, 'Let me try ninety-nine cents for another thirty days and see how that goes.' It actually went really well, so I kept it at that. It was the sales that told me it was the right thing to do."

If you are using the paid download monetization method and want to play it safe, you probably want to stick with the crowd and choose a lower price point. If you are wavering back and forth on which price point to start at, go with the higher one. This gives you two main advantages: One, you might find that the app is a big hit. By charging $1.99 over 99 cents, you have essentially doubled your profits. If the downloads are rolling in, then you know you have priced it right and can just sit back and count your money.

If, on the other hand, downloads are few and far between, you now have the option of lowering the price to attract new customers. Price lowering is a popular strategy many developers build into their pricing strategy from the start. For example, a pricing strategy may be to charge $1.99 for the first six to nine months and then lower the price to 99 cents after that, to try and get a renewed sales bump.

Lowering the price does two things: First, it frees up the app to be purchased by a new set of users. Some smartphone and tablet owners are adamant that they won't spend more than $1 on any app. Lowering the price to 99 cents puts it in their price range, which hopefully will be a boost to sales.

Additionally, lowering the price will get your app on widely read lists that highlight which apps are now on sale or have had their price dropped. A large number of users read those lists, like those on ioSnoops (www.iosnoops.com/iphone-ipad-apps-on-sale) or AppShopper (http://appshopper.com). This is an easy way to drum up free publicity for your app and, hopefully, to reinvigorate sales.

By starting out at just 99 cents, you run the risk of having no pricing options should consumer interest be low. If you aren't getting the number of downloads you would like, your only price-lowering choice is to give it away for free. If you switch from a paid to a free app, you do have the option of adding in-app advertising to try to turn a profit.

Lowering the price from 99 cents to free is also a way to help build consumers for the future. By letting mobile device users download the app at no cost, you are putting your product into the hands of that many more users. Those who enjoy the app may be more inclined to purchase a future offering you may have. Anything to build up your brand and credibility will help you moving forward.

Pricing In-App Purchases

If you are using in-app purchasing, your pricing decisions should really be based on the value the consumers will be getting for their money. Because what you can sell via in-app purchasing is so expansive, so too are the in-app purchase price points.

For example, if you develop a mobile app game and want to give users the opportunity to buy three extra lives or access a new level, you might charge 99 cents. You don't want to overcharge, because ideally you want them to feel they are getting value for what they're buying so they will come back and buy from you again. Ideally, the user will keep playing the game and keep buying more lives and wanting to play new levels. So, while the in-app purchase might seem cheap, if you get one user to buy five in-app purchases, you are significantly reducing the number of overall downloads you will need to make some money.

A good rule of thumb is that if your in-app purchase is something you want users to buy regularly, 99 cents is a good price point. If it is something that users would only purchase once, you have a better chance of convincing a smartphone or tablet owner to spend a little extra money. For example, if you have a free app that includes in-app advertising, one option is to have an in-app purchase option that would remove all the ads for users who pay the price. Because this purchase would remove ads forever, you have more flexibility in pricing above 99 cents. For this, you may charge $2.99 or $3.99.

Additionally, you will want to charge more if you are offering a subscription-based type of in-app purchase. For example, if you have developed an app about your favorite sports team, you may offer a subscription for special "insider stories" that aren't available to those not willing to pay for it. For this access, you might charge $4.99 to $9.99 a month, depending on how valuable you think these extra offerings are.

North Dakota–based app developer Brandon Medenwald says that for his Simple In/Out app, which is designed as a way for employees to seamlessly and effortlessly check in and out from their work locations, in-app purchasing made the most sense. The app is offered for free inside the Apple App and Google Play Stores, with users expected to pay a monthly fee for the actual service.

Medenwald says he and the app's codevelopers had significant internal debates over pricing because the app and service were originally free to generate interest.

"At that point, any pricing seems like a lot," Medenwald says. "Ultimately, what won out was inexpensive pricing. We did do some research on our competitors, but in our case, it was tough, because no one was doing exactly what we were doing. There were other digital in/out boards, but nobody had solved the problem with GeoFencing the way we had solved the problem, so it was hard to understand the value. So we came up with what we thought we would be willing to pay without thinking very hard about it. We made it something so small that no one would think twice."

After much debate, Medenwald and his team settled on charging $5 a month for their cheapest plan, which supported ten users. Their thinking was that the price would be cheap enough where people wouldn't object—but that wasn't a dead-on assumption.

"It ends up being false, because plenty of people don't want to pay for anything on their phone," he says. "Getting them over that hump is difficult, and there are certain people who are never willing to pay you a dime."

What they did find was that once they were able to convert a user into a paying customer, charging them more in the future hasn't been a problem.

"Once you have gotten someone over that hump and they've decided they are going to give you money, then whether it is five, ten, or fifteen dollars, at that point in time it doesn't much matter. Adding a couple extra dollars here and there isn't the end of the world," he says.

So while they started at $5 a month, they have since raised their prices twice, and now charge $9.99 for the cheapest plan and $200 a month for the most expensive plan.

Medenwald credits their strategy of initially offering the app and its services for free, as well as the decision to continue that strategy for businesses with three users or fewer, is what helped them transform nonpaying customers into those willing to pay $10 or $20 a month for the service.

"That ended up being a big deal," Medenwald says. "Letting people understand exactly what to expect helps us out a lot in terms of getting people over the hump. But it is still a challenge, and probably our biggest challenge to date. It isn't the easiest thing in the world. We try to help people out by providing the free plan, and by providing great customer support. When someone e-mails us, we try to return that e-mail within twenty minutes."

As you start to zero in on a price, keep in mind that this is your first app, and, just like with every other step, there is going to be a learning curve. More than likely, you are going to need to play with your price point, and you have the flexibility to do so.

In the end, the only true way to know if your price is on target is to put your app in one of the app stores and see what the consumer response is. If you've researched your competitors and completed your break-even calculations, pick a price and see what happens. While price is a big factor as to whether or not a mobile device owner downloads your app, it's not the only one. Your next step is getting the word out about your app, because unless people know about it, they won't know to download it. And that means it won't make a bit of difference if you used a paid download or in-app purchasing strategy or decided to charge $1.99 over 99 cents.

Chapter Recap

Before you can release your app into the Apple or Android marketplaces, you need to determine how you are going to profit. Here are the most important things to consider when setting your price:

- Pricing strategy: You have three options: paid downloads, in-app purchasing, or in-app advertising. Each option has pros and cons and has a different value depending on the type of app. Be sure to use the method that will work best with your app.

- Competitors: When setting your price, spend some time researching what other developers are charging for comparable apps. You want to make sure your app is in line with what others are charging. If it's priced too high, you won't get as many downloads as you're hoping for; if it's priced too low, you'll miss out on the chance to make a larger profit.

- Break-even: While this figure can't be the only driver in setting your price, you need to calculate how much money it is going to take at each price point to break even. If you don't take this into consideration, your app may never become profitable.

- Paid downloads: If you have an app that people are clamoring for and won't think twice about paying for, this strategy might work best. However, remember to make the price comparable to any competitors' apps, or else you'll run the risk of falling by the wayside. If you are using the paid download strategy, your best bet is to price the app at either $1.99 or 99 cents.

- **In-app purchasing:** This is currently the most profitable method, but it only works if you have something of value to offer users. If you have features, functions, or digital content worth locking up for only those willing to pay for it, in-app purchasing can work for you. Unlike paid downloads, where it is best to keep the price point low, the pricing for in-app purchasing can vary based on what the user is getting for their money.

- **In-app advertising:** In-app ads are a common way for developers to make money off free apps. To use this strategy, find an online ad network that will provide the ads and tools needed to display them on your site. The ad network you partner with pays you based on how many users see and click on the ads. The pricing varies by each provider, so it is important to research the options to make sure you are getting the best deal and an ad network that is trustworthy and not selling users' private info.

- **Combination:** While each of these pricing strategies can work well on their own, they can also be used in tandem. Many free apps include in-app ads and then offer an in-app purchase to remove them. Additionally, if you think you have an app people really want, with extra features worth charging for, there is nothing stopping you from combining the paid download and in-app purchasing methods.

- **Flexibility:** None of the prices you pick are set in stone. Take advantage of that flexibility and adjust prices if needed. When your sales become fluid, you know you are pricing it right. If you haven't reached that stage, switch up the pricing to see how consumers react.

11 Marketing Your App in Mobile App Stores

Properly marketing your mobile app could be the most important stage of the whole development process. Yes, coming up with an idea that is going to appeal to consumers and building an app that looks and functions as advertised are vital. But if no one knows your app exists, you aren't going to make money. Always remember your end goal of building a successful and profitable business. Your first app needs to lay the groundwork for that, and it won't make money without a significant effort to promote to the masses.

Marketing your app needs to be a multipronged process that includes both in-store and out-of-store tactics. For in-store promotion—meaning, what mobile device owners will see when they search for your app in any of the app marketplaces—you need to have an appealing name, eye-catching logo, and thoughtful description.

Naming Your Mobile App

While the majority of the marketing work takes place once the app has been released for public consumption, picking out a name really should be done much earlier. You want to come up with it as soon as possible, so you can ensure that a matching web domain name is also available. Developers agree that having an online site featuring a matching domain name and social media accounts that match the mobile app's name are critical. For example, if you have an app named "BestAppEver," then you should also have a website with an address of www.bestappever.com, a Facebook account of BestAppEver, and a Twitter handle of @BestAppEver. You want everything associated with your app and its brand easily identifiable and connected.

As soon as you come up with your app's name, you want to immediately reserve a web domain and social media handles of the same name. If the name you want is already taken, then you might want to consider coming up with a new app name.

Finding a name that's free in all the app marketplaces and has an available web domain can be a difficult process, so it's best to get started as soon as possible. However, while you are free to secure a web domain and social media accounts with the name, you don't want to formally submit them for approval until your app is nearing completion, especially if you are building an iOS app for the Apple App Store.

To prevent mobile app developers from securing names they don't have any intention of ever using—commonly referred to as "name squatting"—Apple requires that you submit your app for approval within 180 days of officially registering the name. If you don't submit the app for approval within the specified time frame, Apple will delete the name and not allow it to be used with your account again.

The most important factor when choosing a mobile app name is finding one that isn't being used. First off, if the name is exactly the same as what is already being used, the app stores have the right to remove your app for trademark or copyright violations. The last thing you want is to invest months of your time and thousands of dollars into the app's development, only to have it be barred from ever being sold because of the name.

Similar to its approval process, Apple is much more restrictive with its name requirements than the other app marketplaces. Unlike the Apple App Store, you will find apps with the same name in the Google Play Store. While Apple shuts down any possible trademark infringement from the start, developers must file a grievance with Google to get an app removed from the Google Play Store they feel is violating their copyright or trademark protection.

One important thing to remember when naming an Android app is that it cannot include the word "Android" on its own. For example, your app is not allowed to be named "Android BestAppEver." If you wanted to use Android in your app's name, you would need to call it "BestAppEver for Android." This rule also applies to the Amazon Appstore. If you want to use Kindle or Kindle Fire in your app's name, it can only be done if using the words "for" or "to," such as "BestAppEver for Kindle Fire."

It is possible to have an Android app with the same name as another app, but this is something you should try to avoid. You don't want there to be any confusion over which app is yours. You want your app to stand out from all others that are out there, not just in terms of functionality, but from a name standpoint as well.

However, as I mentioned previously, choosing the name must be done in tandem with securing similar names for a web domain and social media accounts. Naming your app, creating a website, and being active on social media are all important to your marketing efforts. To effectively promote your app, you need your branding to be cohesive. You don't want confusion from consumers if the website or social media handles affiliated with your app don't match up. All three need to be synonymous with each other.

In addition to making sure the name works across your marketing channels, you also want to ensure that the app name helps to describe what the app does. For example, if you have a recipe app, you want to figure out how to include the words "recipes" or "food" in the name so consumers know what the app is about as soon as they see it. More than likely, they won't spend time trying to figure out what your app does if the name doesn't explicitly say. Just like with your pricing, don't give the shopper a reason to buy something else. Make sure your name leaves little to the imagination regarding what your app is and what it does.

Other factors you want to consider when naming your app include its length and pronounceability. Ideally, you want your app name to be as short as possible and easy to read and say. A confusing or unclear name may give off a bad first impression, and is the only impetus consumers need to download from someone else.

From a presentation standpoint, Apple recommends keeping the name to no more than twenty-five characters, and not including descriptive words in the name. For example, with our fictitious BestAppEver, you wouldn't want to call it "BestApp Ever—All the Tools a Mobile Device Owner Needs." Instead, keep the name short—"BestAppEver"—and then include any explanations in your app's description inside the various app stores.

TeliApp's founder, Josh Weiss—whose apps include Love Struck, Trust Me, and iBox Remote File Access—believes that the key to any successful app name is making sure it explains what the app does, because that is how it will end up in users' search results.

"Usually the best names are the ones that accurately describe what you are doing in two words or less—preferably one," Weiss says. "It has to be something that is unique, and it has to be something that's obvious, because you want it to appear in the search results. A lot of times people will stumble upon apps that they never really were looking for, but they were looking for something in that category, and your app popped up."

Weiss says that making sure the name reflected what smartphone and tablet owners would be searching for was a key factor in deciding to use the name iBox Remote File Access for their app, which allows users to access their Windows computers via their Apple or Android smartphones. Weiss says they were originally going to name the app iView, because you are remotely viewing your files, but went with iBox because they knew there was a greater chance consumers would be searching for an app with the word "box" in it.

"We thought, maybe for marketing purposes, people might be looking for Dropbox, and type in the word 'box,' and now we're going to pop up also," he says.

Once you settle on a name, you need to start focusing on the rest of your in-store marketing, which includes writing a thorough product description that features the perfect screenshots to showcase your apps.

Product Description

The second piece of your in-store marketing is your product description page. This is the page that mobile device owners go to in order to download an app from any of the app marketplaces. While each marketplace is slightly different, this page features

Online Resources: App and Web Domain Name Generators

If you are struggling to come up with a clever app name that is going to resonate with consumers, there are a number of online resources available to help. "Name generator" services help to devise names for both mobile apps and web domains. Not only will they help you come up with the names, but they will also ensure that no one else has taken them. Even if you don't end up choosing a suggested name, it could bolster your creative process. The services, some of which are free and some of which charge a fee, include:

- DomainGroovy—http://domaingroovy.com/website-name-generator
- Dot-o-mator—www.dotomator.com
- NameBoy—http://nameboy.com
- NameFind—www.namefind.com
- Panabee—www.panabee.com

a detailed product description and screenshots of your app. Screenshots are basically pictures of what the device's screen looks like when your app is in use.

This is your opportunity to tell and show consumers everything there is to know about your app. You want to hold nothing back with your written description. By reading it, readers should know exactly what the app has to offer and how it will function. While your app name and logo—the third piece of the in-store marketing puzzle—are essential tools used to lure potential customers in, it is the product description and screenshots that are really going to close the sale.

Budgets are tight these days, making shoppers less frivolous with their money than they might have once been. So while you might only be asking them to spend a dollar or two, they will still want to make sure they are getting value for their money. To do that, they are going to read up on your app to see what it has to offer.

That's why, just like any good news story, you want those first few sentences—your lead—to really pack a punch to draw consumers in. With time at a premium for most mobile device owners, they'll only read the first couple of sentences and look at the pictures. If those aren't telling and showing them what they want to hear and see, they will quickly, and without a second thought, move on to something else.

When writing product descriptions, Apple, which limits descriptions to 4,000 words, encourages developers to always take into account the following: the Apple App Store screen size, so they know what shoppers will be seeing when the description is showing; to use bulleted lists to highlight main features; and to eliminate any unnecessary white space or any lengthy website URLs. Additionally, they advise that you only include reviews and testimonials at the end, if at all.

Weiss says developers run a huge risk of seriously damaging their reputation by not being as fully descriptive as possible.

"You need to be as descriptive and honest as possible," Weiss says. "You don't want to give customers an opportunity to think that you in any way misled them. You want to be as descriptive as possible so there is no room for them to come back to you and say, 'Hey, I only downloaded this because I thought it had this, and it doesn't.' "

That's why his iBox app description doesn't hide the fact that it only works with Windows and currently doesn't support media streaming. Instead, the description explicitly states that it doesn't work with Macs, and that while media streaming isn't supported now, it will be in future versions.

Weiss says misleading consumers will mean losing them as potential future customers and critically damaging your app's reputation in the marketplaces. Because users have the ability to rate and review the apps they purchase, Weiss says it is vital to make sure they don't leave a lasting negative review for others to read.

"Users have more power than you know," he says. "They can go back and give you a negative rating that is going to torpedo sales from today until forever. That's why there is this need to be descriptive, honest, open, forthcoming, and as personal as possible."

Just be honest and straightforward. In theory, you are going to be proud of what you've developed, so there is no need to lie or mislead users about what the app might or might not contain. When getting ready to write your description, jot some notes down first about the app and the things you like best about it.

Start off with the basics about what the app does. Include any basic functions and any upgraded features. Be specific in talking about what each function and feature does, to help remove any confusion from the reader's mind about your app's intended purposes.

Also, don't be afraid to talk about why someone would want or need the app. This is your chance to put on your best salesman face in order to tell readers exactly why your app is for them. This is your one chance to convince smartphone and tablet owners to purchase your app, so don't leave anything out that might be persuasive to someone. Even if you think a feature isn't that important, if it can be an enticement to just one person to download the app, then it is worth including.

If you aren't a good writer, get someone to help who is. If your description has bad grammar and spelling, customers are going to be extremely wary of buying anything from you. This is a business venture, so you need to represent yourself in a professional manner at all times. A poorly written description screams "amateur hour," and will leave readers wondering what the app itself will be like if the writing isn't even enticing. Most people won't be willing to spend their money to find out.

If writing professionally isn't your cup of tea—and it's okay if it isn't—you should consider hiring someone to do it for you. This isn't the only writing project that you and your company will need to do. You are also going to need professionally written press releases and website content, so don't think you'll be all set if you can just cobble together a description. You won't.

The good news is, just like mobile app programmers, there are thousands of freelance writers with the skills necessary to write not only your app descriptions, but your press releases, website content, and any other writing need that may arise as well.

You can find freelance writers for jobs like these in many of the same online places your freelance app programmers are found. Freelancer, Elance, and oDesk are all places through which you can hire a freelance writer. Freelance writers often charge an hourly rate—anywhere from $20 to $100 an hour—or charge by word count, such as 10 cents a word.

While this will be an added expense, the cost will be worth it if it helps to portray your app and company in a more positive and professional light. If you can't afford a freelancer, find a friend or family member who can help—someone you know who is a good writer and would probably be willing to help out for dinner or a few beers. In the end, it doesn't matter who is doing the writing, as long as what it says reads clearly and sounds smart.

Product Screenshots

In addition to your written description, your product pages in the Apple App Store, Google Play Store, and Amazon Kindle Store give you the option of including screenshots of your app. This takes a bit of pressure off the task of painting a picture with words.

Just like with the description, the screenshots should accurately portray the app and its functions, and in no way should mislead anyone about what the app is capable of.

Each app store has its own requirements for and restrictions on the screenshots that can be used. Apple, which limits product pages to five different screenshots, recommends that developers use the best shot first, omit any additional graphics or borders, and try to focus the shots on what users will experience when using your app.

In the Google Play Store, you can use between two and eight screenshots. Google advises developers to crop out any of the navigation buttons at the bottom of the app in the screenshot. In addition, the screenshots must be between 320 and 3840 pixels.

For Amazon, developers can include between three and ten screenshots on their product detail page. The screenshots must be either 1024 x 600 pixels or 800 x 480 pixels, and be in PNG or JPEG format. In addition, if your screenshots show how a user's personal information might be used in the app, Amazon encourages developers to use fictional details.

Both Google and Amazon also offer options to include videos on their product pages. Google lets users link a short YouTube video to their product pages, while Amazon lets developers post up to five different videos directly on their pages.

App Icons

Another key aspect of the in-store marketing is the app icon. This is shown on your product page, and it is also the icon shown on the user's smartphone or tablet after it has been downloaded.

The icon is what helps you make a great first impression. Often, mobile device owners simply look at an app icon and name when deciding if it is worth downloading. If the app doesn't make an impact, smartphone and tablet owners are quickly going to zero in on those that do.

There are several design elements that developers must consider when creating their app icons. The most important is size. Each app store requires various sizes of each app. The larger versions are put into the app store, while the smallest ones are typically found on smartphones. The trick is making sure the icon looks exactly the same in each version, regardless of size and the device on which it is being viewed.

That means you really need to understand the pixel requirements for each size to ensure that the icon doesn't change in appearance when made larger or smaller. Apple requires developers to provide different icon sizes based on the device and where it will be seen. Here are the specific pixel requirements for each device:

Where the App Is Seen	iPhone 5 and iPod Touch (5th Generation)	High-Resolution iPhone and iPod Touch	iPhone and iPod Touch	High-Resolution iPad	iPad
On the device	114 x 114	114 x 114	57 x 57	144 x 144	72 x 72
In the app store	1024 x 1024	1024 x 1024	512 x 512	1024 x 1024	512 x 512

Android developers need to make sure they check with each of the different stores for specific pixel requirements. Google Play requires icons seen on the apps to be 48 x 48, while those seen in the Google Play Store need to be 512 x 512.

For Amazon, developers must submit icons that are 114 x 114 pixels for Kindle owners to see on their device, and icons that are 512 x 512 pixels to be used both on product description pages and in search results.

Regardless of which app store you plan to be in, each requires that the icons you submit are provided in a PNG format. It is important to remember this, as submitting them in the wrong format, such as JPEG, is a quick way to get your app rejected.

Because the icon appears larger in some places and smaller in others, another design element to factor in is text. While using words might seem like a good idea to help strengthen an icon's impact, it's best to avoid them altogether. While the text might be easily readable in a larger format, the same probably can't be said for the smaller versions.

App icons on a smartphone are pretty small. It's highly likely that most people would be unable to read what you've written there. It also adds unnecessary clutter. Remember, your app's name is going to be directly under that icon on the device it has been downloaded to, making any text within the icon itself repetitive.

A key to designing any good icon is to make sure it fits in with the app. The look and feel of the icon should be just an extension of the app. The same design elements (e.g., colors, textures, etc.) you use in your app should be extended to your icon.

For example, Washington, D.C., developer Manne Darby's SuChef app has an orange icon with a big white chef's hat. The icon also has some gold stars and streaking effects. When you launch SuChef, those colors, effects, and the hat are all exactly the same in the app.

Darby says he had no design experience, but he found a freelance artist on Elance who was willing to help him out. Darby says he gave the designer $50, and several days later he had a choice of icons to choose from.

Online Resources: App Icons

It doesn't take the next Picasso to design an app icon. For those who feel they can't create an icon on their own but don't have the money for a graphic designer, there are several online resources to help. There are a number of app icon generators that help developers create icons for a nominal fee. Many of these resources are free. Here are five app icon sites that can help you make a great first impression:

- Easy App Icon Maker—http://graphicriver.net/item/easy-app-icon-maker/2563742
- Icon Slayer—www.gieson.com/Library/projects/utilities/icon_slayer/#.Uc4e6eukCeo
- Img2icns—www.img2icnsapp.com
- iOS 7 App Icon Kit—http://medialoot.com/item/iphone-app-icon-kit
- MakeAppIcon—http://makeappicon.com

"I had an idea of what I wanted, and I pitched it to a [freelance] design company, and they came back with several designs over the course of a few days," Darby says.

Because this icon is so important, it wasn't a detail Darby just wanted to throw together at the last minute. He says he started creating his icon months before the app was ever close to being finished so he could use it in his early branding efforts, which included launching the app's website well before the app's release, to start creating some hype and building up some brand awareness.

"The reason the icon was developed months ago was because at the same time, we were developing the website and putting information on there, so we wanted to know what the face of SuChef was going to be," he says.

Other design elements to consider when designing your icon, which many developers do on their own using Photoshop, include making sure the look and feel appeals to your target audience (pink elephants on a sports app probably won't do the trick), and ensuring that colors, textures, and effects are geared toward the user most likely to download the app.

Additionally, you want to be original. While it might seem like creating an icon similar to the competition's would be an easy way to earn some downloads, it really isn't. In the end, you just end up confusing your users and giving them a reason to look at you like a slimy used-car salesman.

Create an icon that's original and sets you apart from everyone else. Remember, this icon isn't just something used to attract new customers; it is also going to be something those who download it see each and every day on their devices.

The icon is a way for you to strengthen brand awareness with smartphone and tablet owners on a daily basis. If it doesn't match up with the app or look professional, users are going to think the same applies to your app. Don't give them a reason to think your app and your brand are anything but top of the line.

Keywords

Once you finalize everything mobile device owners will see when they visit your product pages in the app stores, you need to make sure they have a good way to actually find you. This final piece of the in-store marketing puzzle happens behind the scenes. Choosing the proper keywords is imperative, and can easily mean the difference between having a successful and profitable app and one that sits in the various app stores collecting dust. This is not something you want to just gloss over. Taking the time to figure out which keywords are going to drive traffic to your app is vital.

Keywords help Apple, Google, Amazon, and any of the other app marketplaces determine which apps pop up when certain terms are searched. You want your keywords to include words that someone who would want your app would be searching for.

For example, if you have an app about cupcakes that includes demonstrations and recipes, keywords might include:

- Cupcake recipes
- How to make a cupcake
- Making a cupcake
- Making cupcakes
- Cool-looking cupcakes
- Best-tasting cupcakes, etc.

The key is striking the proper balance between keywords that are commonly searched for and those that won't lump you in with too many similar apps. Using keywords that are too common will make it harder for users to find you when they come searching.

As with all the other steps of the process, Apple carefully reviews the keywords developers choose to make sure they properly align with the app. Keywords that Apple will reject include objectionable terms, trademarked terms, company or product names, celebrity names, and irrelevant terms.

The process is a bit different for Google. For Google Play, your keywords need to be included within the text of your app description. This is important to remember when writing your app description, as it will require a little more effort to ensure that all of the keywords you want are included.

Amazon has a number of keyword restrictions, including not using the app title, category, vendor, or developer name, because these will automatically be picked up from the app's product page. Developers are also asked not to use the words "free" or "free app," even if the app is free, as well as other app names, vague terms that aren't relevant to the app, and all capital letters, exclamation marks, question marks, and symbols.

Character Limits

There are a few things to remember when choosing your keywords. The first is that you only have a certain number of characters available with Apple and Amazon. For Apple it is 100, and for Amazon it is 249. (Remember, your keywords are included in your production description and app title for Google Play.) This limits the number of keywords, each of which needs to be separated by a comma, that you can have—which means that picking the right ones is crucial.

This is especially true of the Apple App Store, where keywords cannot be changed once the app is submitted. The only times Apple allows developers to update their keywords is when they provide an actual updated version of the app itself. Each time you submit an updated version of the app, you also must include a new set of keywords. While these can be the same ones you have previously used, this also gives you the opportunity to add some new ones if you don't think they are helping to drive the right amount of traffic to your app.

Thinking about the User

Another factor to take into consideration when choosing keywords is to think more about the user and less about the app. You need to put yourself in the mind of a smartphone or tablet owner who is searching for apps. What words and phrases are they going to be typing that are related to your app? Research has shown that the majority of users use search terms pertaining to function rather than a specific name. This means you have to think hard about the functions your app offers and how people might go about searching for something like that.

If we go back to our cupcake app, we would want to use not only terms related to cupcakes, but also those that involve cooking, baking, or making desserts. Your app could fill a need for all those tasks.

While this process can be tedious, there are some online resources that can help you to not only come up with keywords, but all of your search engine optimization (SEO) needs, as well. The most commonly used free tool, Google AdWords, can be used to come up with keywords for any of the marketplaces. This free service lets you type in words and phrases to see what might be a good fit. Included with each term are details, such as how many people are searching for those terms on Google each month. While these metrics might not give you the perfect set of keywords, they will get you thinking on the right track, at no cost.

For those willing to invest in some SEO, there are a number of services that can help. Not only will they help you to come up with an optimized set of keywords specific for your app, but many also offer a number of other services, including providing analytics on how your app is performing and statistics on your competitors. Among those offering such services, which can range from $15 to $400 a month, are www .appcodes.com, https://appnique.com, https://sensortower.com, and https://search-man.com.

Many of these services offer free trials that include limited access to different features. If you are considering this option, the free trials are a good way to determine if you think you would benefit from these services. This will be an added expense, so you need to weigh carefully whether or not this is something you really can't do on your own. Because keywords are so important, it might be worth spending some extra money.

Once you have all your in-store marketing, name, description, screenshots, icons, and keywords nailed down, you can turn your attention to marketing your app externally.

Chapter Recap

In-store marketing is one of the most critical aspects of the entire app development process. When smartphone or tablet owners search for your app, you want them to easily find it and, when they do, be impressed with what they see. To do that, you need to focus on the following four areas:

1. Name: When naming your app, you want to pick something that is going be short, easy to pronounce, and relevant to your app. Choose a name whose meaning people will instantly recognize. Also, be sure that the name you choose has an available domain name and social media handles. This helps to build up your branding across all avenues.

2. Product description: This is your chance to let users know exactly what they can expect from your app. Give a clear and thorough description that doesn't mislead readers into thinking the app does something it can't. Included should

be screenshots that show off the app and complement the written description. When they are done reading and looking at the screenshots, smartphone and tablet owners should have a full, clear picture of your app.

3. Icon: The icon serves two purposes: attracting new customers who see it when searching for similar apps, and strengthening brand recognition with current customers who see the icon on their phones and tablets each day. You want to design something that is simple, yet detailed enough to instantly let those looking at it know what the app

12 Marketing Your App Outside of the App Stores

While a large majority of your app downloads will come from people searching in the different app stores, you can't forget about targeting everyone else. Not every smartphone and tablet owner spends his or her time searching for new apps in the app stores. Many are turned on to new apps by recommendations from friends or family, reading reviews online, or seeing news about the app in their social media feeds.

That's why it is important to get word of your app out to the masses. Some of these tasks can be done on your own, through things like social media accounts and your app website, while for other tasks, you'll need help from others, like getting reviewed in a magazine or app blog. The first step is setting up an online home for your app that is outside of the app stores.

Creating a Website for Your App

To build an online presence for your app, you need to start making an online imprint. This is done in many different ways, one of which is creating a website for the app. While you may already have a site for your business, you want a separate one for your app that will serve as its online home.

The website will be a place where users can learn more about your app and what it does, and it can drive more users to the app stores where they can buy it. The first step, as we talked about earlier, is picking the site's domain name. As discussed, the name should be the same as your app's title. This will help to build consistent branding for your app and company.

While building a website can be an easy task, aided by numerous online tools, it can also be difficult, depending on how robust you want the site to be. Any of these routes are going to cost more money; the question is how much you want to invest.

Online sites like GoDaddy or iPage give users all the tools they need to build their own page for as little as a dollar per month, while professional web designers can charge tens of thousands of dollars. At first, you are probably best served going with a cheaper option. If the app really starts to take off, you may want to invest down the road in a website that is a bit more advanced, but when just starting out, something simple will work just fine.

We aren't going to get into the details of web design, because that could be a book entirely on its own, but it is important to know what every good mobile app companion website should have. Most important, the website is another way to show off your app.

Product Description

You want to show off every aspect, leaving no stone unturned. Unlike the restrictions that Apple, Google, and Amazon place on developers when writing their in-store descriptions, there are no limitations when building your own website.

Again, this isn't a place to mislead consumers on what you have to offer. Be straightforward, but also be thorough. This is an opportunity to show off the app actually being used. Include screenshots and videos, as well as user testimonials and reviews. Using a variety of different mediums—text, photos, graphics, and video—ensures that users know exactly what they would be getting if they downloaded your app.

Badges

In addition to the thorough description and app demonstrations, you also must include a way for visitors to quickly get to your app inside the app marketplaces. Apple, Google Play, and Amazon all allow developers to include a predesigned link that says "Download on the App Store" or "Get it on Google Play." These are preapproved "badges" that all developers are encouraged to include on their app websites.

These badges are key; by including them, you are giving mobile device owners a direct link to your app in the Apple, Google, and Amazon marketplaces. These links make sure that those interested in your app don't have to go anywhere else for it. Without these links, a smartphone or tablet owner interested in downloading your app would have to exit the web browser and open up the app store.

From there, users would have to search for your app. At that point, you are risking another app popping up in their search results that piques their interest more. Unless they search for your app by its exact name, other apps will come up in their search results. Including the badge on your website guarantees that they won't find something they like better while trying to find your app in the app stores.

By clicking on these badges, mobile devices owners are taken straight to your product description page inside the app store. From there, they can download your app.

Contact Page

In addition to the description and app store links, the third key component to any professional website is a way for visitors to contact you. This gives app users or potential customers the chance to ask you specific questions about how the app functions.

It also gives users a way—other than a bad review—to contact you about a problem they run into after downloading the app. While no one wants to hear someone complain, it does provide several benefits.

First, if the app isn't performing up to par, you need to know. You don't want your app not working as expected. You want to fix changes as quickly as possible, so every new user isn't running into the same problems. The longer it takes for you to find out about a problem, the more unsatisfied customers you are going to have on your hands.

Without a contact page that offers either a contact form or e-mail address to reach you, the only choice a user has to voice their frustrations over a faulty app is to write negative review. You would much rather get a dozen e-mails a month from unhappy customers than just one negative review.

App-store reviews can make or break any app. The majority of mobile device owners will read reviews of an app before they spend money on it. If your product page is filled with other users complaining about how the app is constantly crashing or not living up to its billing, there is no way potential customers are going to download it. Why would they give up their hard-earned money for something numerous others are criticizing?

Social Media Links

Another key aspect of your app's website should be direct links to your social media accounts. This website is serving as an online hub for your app. From this website, your customers and potential customers should be able to reach all of your touchpoints with a single click of the mouse.

Facebook, Twitter, and Google+ allow website owners to include icon links straight to a user's handle. It is important to take advantage of those tools so users who are interested in joining in on a conversation about the app have a simple way to do so.

As with everything throughout this process, you want to make things as simple as possible for the customer. This is just another way of doing so.

Blog

Another feature some developers include on their website is a blog. This serves multiple purposes. First, it is a way for you to establish yourself as an expert in your field so people can trust that your app is going to fill their needs. Remember, this isn't about being an expert on apps; it's about being an expert on the subject that your app is about.

For example, Manne Darby, developer of the SuChef app, has been able to position himself as an authority on saving time and money, which he feels is the primary purpose of the app. So he hasn't just pigeonholed himself into talking about grocery shopping or cooking dinner. By talking about broader themes like saving time and money, Darby is able to use his blog to expand his audience.

Now, not only will people find his app and blog when they are searching for ways to simplify their dinner preparation process, but they may also find him when looking for ways to save time or money. Through his blog posts and website, Darby has a chance to obtain new customers who may not have been looking for an app originally.

Search Engine Optimization (SEO)

The blog also helps with SEO, which is how Internet users find things they are looking for when searching online. SEO is used by Google, Yahoo, and the other search engines in determining the results that pop up each time a visitor makes a search on the site. The better your SEO, the higher your site will pop up in the search results.

"It's the process of attempting to get your website to return higher up in search engines when people search for terms associated with your product," says Tim Tagaris, an online marketing expert who has served as a new media and digital director for a number of political candidates, as well as the Service Employees International Union. "The higher up on the page a search engine returns your results, the more likely you are to get a click and a chance to convert that visitor into a 'buyer.'"

Research has shown that three-quarters of Internet searchers never scroll past the first page of their results, and that the very first result receives more than 50 percent of the user clicks. That means if you are halfway down page three, the vast majority of people looking for your app or something similar to it will never find it.

One way SEO is determined is by how many links your site has and is linked to. Your blog is an excellent way to include links to other internal things on your site, like your download page or previous blog postings, and to external sites. All of these links can help in boosting SEO. When it comes to SEO, every little bit helps. So, while a blog posting might not garner that many reads, it does have the potential to pay off in other ways.

Tagaris offers several simple ways developers can start to boost their SEO rankings:

- The first and most important thing you can do is to pick search terms that will direct your target users to your site when they're browsing online. Try to pick keywords that provide a good balance between terms for which there is a ton of competition and terms that no one is searching for.
- Once you have selected the appropriate keywords, use them often on your website. Also, use them prominently, such as by bolding them and putting them in the site's title tag.
- Use Google Analytics to track which keywords people are using to get to your site, and which result in the most downloads.
- Keep your site updated.

In addition to serving as your app's online hub, the website will also be a place to cross-promote other apps you may develop in the future. For each new app you develop, you will also want to develop a corresponding website. All the websites can cross-link with each other, driving new business to each, as well as to your company page, should you reach that point.

New York City developer and founder of app development company Problemio, Alex Genadinik, says that at first he didn't see much need for a website for his series of business start-up apps, called "Business Plan & Start," "Small Business & Start-Up Ideas," "Marketing and Advertising Plan," and "Funding and Fund-Raising Ideas." He was already generating a large amount of traffic solely from users finding his app on their own in each of the app stores he was in—Apple, Google Play, Amazon, and Nook.

However, as other developers began releasing apps similar to his, Genadinik had to find a way to boost his consumer interest, so he turned to building up his online presence.

"I had figured out how to market in the app stores very well," Genadinik says. "But in the last year, the landscape became more competitive. Getting traffic through the web and social media became much more important."

Regardless of what the website contains, the key is making sure it looks great, Genadinik says. He says the site is an extension of the app, and if the site doesn't look good, smartphone and tablet owners won't expect much from the app.

"In the app world, design is a must," Genadinik says. "Design is a sign of professionalism, and professionalism is a sign of whether or not you are serious or not. People don't want to see bad designs. They want to see something polished. And while bringing people into your site is one thing, it's another to try and actually convert them into clients. And for that you need [the website] to be polished and professional."

Great SEO can play a pivotal role in an app's success, so you won't want to wait until the last minute to launch your website. Instead of unveiling the website on the same day the app is released, the best strategy is to launch the site several months ahead of time to start building both SEO and hype.

Online Resources: Registering and Building a Website

Developers have a wide variety of choices when it comes to choosing where to register their domain name. Most of these online services also provide assistance in actually building the website itself. They include:

- Bluehost—www.bluehost.com
- Domain.com—www.domain.com
- FatCow—www.fatcow.com
- GoDaddy—www.godaddy.com
- iPage—www.ipage.com
- Just Host—www.justhost.com
- Network Solutions—www.networksolutions.com
- 1&1—www.1and1.com
- Register.com—www.register.com
- Web.com—www.web.com

Launching Your Website

At this point, you don't need to have a completed app with fully developed screen-shots. All you need when launching the website prior to an app's release is a few details and a release countdown. Because you won't have an exact date of when the app will be released, you can be vague and say "Coming Summer 2014." As the app gets closer to completion and you start to have a better idea of how much longer it will take for completion, and to be approved by the app stores, you can be more specific.

Once your app launches, you will want to add a section to the website for the media. Beyond displaying your press release and any publicity you receive, this section is a place for the media to come and get all the background they need on your app.

Virginia-based app developers Kevin and Diane Hamilton advise all developers to include a website media kit that includes print-quality logos, icons, and screenshots. In addition, Hamilton says a reviewer's guide—which walks readers through the entire app and all of its functions—can also be valuable.

"It's not just a quick tutorial, but it puts the app into context," Kevin Hamilton says. "You want to put it all in a broader context. What we have found is that when [writers] do use these materials, a lot of time you will see almost word-for-word quotes pulled right out of your document. These pitch your side of things. It has been an effective technique."

Once your website is at least partially developed and online, you can expand your marketing efforts to include some social networking strategies.

Social Media

One of the easiest and cheapest ways to promote your app outside of the app stores is via social media. The explosion of Facebook, Twitter, Google+, and other popular social networking sites has given app developers an effective and free way to reach their target audience. Facebook and Twitter are the sites you should focus on first.

Just like with the website, the first step is securing your social media handles. These are the names you will go by on each social networking site, which means you want your handle to mirror your app's name.

While you might already have a personal Facebook and Twitter account, you still need accounts specifically dedicated to the apps. Using your personal social network-ing accounts is not the way to build your app's brand and credibility.

Facebook

For Facebook, sign up for a "Brand or Product" page, rather than a normal individual profile. Unlike your personal account, business pages don't collect friends. Instead, they collect "fans" who "like" the page. Those Facebook users who become fans of your site will see your posts in their newsfeeds, right alongside those of their friends and family.

Once you've signed up for your business page, you can start posting things immediately. Some of the things your business page should include are your app's icon, which needs to be featured as your page's profile picture, and basic information on the app in the "About" section.

Twitter

For Twitter, the 140-character social network, sign up just as you would for a personal account. You want your Twitter name—which always starts with the "@" sign—to match your app's name. Developer Peter Kruger's Rock Lobby Twitter handle, for instance, is @RockLobby. However, because Twitter handles cannot be duplicated, there is a chance your app's name may already be taken. In those cases, your best bet is to include the word app at the end of your Twitter handle. For example, Manne Darby's SuChef app's Twitter handle is @SuChefApp, and Benny Hsu's Photo 365 app's is @Photo365App.

One thing to remember is that Twitter only allows one account per e-mail address, so if you already have a personal account, you will need to get another e-mail address to register your app's account. Once you've signed up, use your app's icon as your main photo, and include a short description of the app and your app's website address.

Other Social Networking Sites

While Facebook and Twitter are the sites you will focus on first, that doesn't mean you can't start securing your handles on some of the other more popular social networking sites, like Google+, Pinterest, and Instagram. Even though you may not be adding content to these regularly, there is nothing wrong with planning ahead to make sure you get the handles that match up with your app's name.

Once you are signed up with each social network, you need to start collecting fans and followers. This can be very slow going at first, so you can't let yourself get frustrated should you not see immediate results.

The first way to start attracting fans and followers is to start following and liking other pages and profiles. Look for other people who are talking about things your app is centered on. If it is a photo app, look for people who are tweeting about taking pictures; or, for a recipe app, look for foodies.

By following and liking others, there is a good chance many will do the same for you in return. If they don't start following you back right away, an easy way to gain their favor is by retweeting one of their tweets or sharing one of their Facebook posts.

Once those people start following, you have now opened yourself up to gaining some of their followers. This gives you a chance to build on your consumer base exponentially with each new follower.

Following and liking and retweeting and sharing is only a first step, however. You also have to give people a reason to keep following you. The key to promoting your app on Facebook—and, really, on any of the social networks—is to not use it solely to encourage the sale of your app. Social networks are designed to drive conversations between people. You want to join in on that conversation rather than purport yourself to be solely an advertiser.

Just like with a blog, you want to use your social networking accounts to talk more about the industry your app fits into rather than just the app itself. To be honest, there are very few people in your social networking circles who will care that you have a new app. You need to bring much more to the table to keep people interested in your social networking feeds—which, in the end, is the only way you will convert some of them into actual customers.

Darby says he started his social media efforts well before the release of his app, creating accounts and joining in on conversations as a way to build up his social network credibility before he had something to sell everyone.

"Months ago, I started following a lot of bloggers that talk about food waste, or saving time, saving money, that are family-oriented, parenting-type bloggers," Darby says. "I followed them to see what they would post. Sometimes I commented if I thought the article was well written or well researched. People are human, and they like to know that they write it well and people are reading it. So, I think it is best to start that way, by following the people you hope to influence. Anyone can be influenced—it is just a matter of time and effectiveness."

Once you build up some followers and start generating some conversations on relevant topics, you can do a little bit of direct app promotion. Your followers can stomach some direct advertising, but give them too much of it and they are quickly going to drop you from their circle of online friends.

In the end, if you want to effectively use social media marketing, you have to do a good job of attracting followers, especially those who can influence others, and you have to keep them engaged. The more you can do that, the more results you will see from your social media efforts.

Expert's View: Social Networking

Brandon Medenwald

As a developer with a strong programming background, Brandon Medenwald, cofounder of Simply Made Apps, says one of his company's biggest challenges has been on the marketing side. To get started, he says they signed up for a host of social networking accounts.

"We have a company page on Facebook, a company page on LinkedIn, a company handle on Twitter, and a company page on Google+," Medenwald says. "We went out and got a bunch of those and started funneling our PR into that. Then we started a blog."

However, for those who think a blog about their app is going to quickly turn into the next Huffington Post or TMZ—currently the most popular blogs on the Internet—Medenwald says to think again. He says few, beyond friends and family, will care about what you're writing at first. Medenwald did it to keep a kind of historical record of what they were working on. Once the app started generating customers, Medenwald says their social networking and blog started to become a little more popular.

Medenwald says he realized their efforts were paying off early on in the sale of the app, when an Australian customer who was upset the app didn't account for time zone differences contacted them via a social network. After fixing the problem by the next day, Medenwald says the user was so happy that she started sharing her positive interactions with Simply Made Apps online.

"Because of that, we ended up with ten or fifteen paying customers from Australia, a place we had never been, all just based on the fact that we had the social media in place. So that's where most of our marketing has come in," he says.

One area in which Medenwald says they didn't find success was spending money for advertising via Google AdWords, Facebook ads, or LinkedIn ads.

"We never saw any of that translate into actual business," he says. "I'm not saying that it can't be successful, but in the beginning, for us, it certainly wasn't. To that point, we no longer dump money into that."

Medenwald says they also struck out trying to host a social media contest. To encourage users to "like" their Facebook page, Simply Made Apps held a contest for a free Kindle Fire. As part of the contest, users who "liked" their Facebook were automatically registered for a chance to win. While harder to track, he says the giveaway, similar to paying for ads, was ineffective. In the end, the contest was a double whammy for Medenwald: It didn't lead to any business, and cost the company extra money in shipping costs when the winner turned out to be from London.

"Ultimately, that didn't turn into anything that we could see either," he says. "We never saw an uptick in sales because of that. So I don't know if we would actually ever do that again."

Since unveiling the app in 2011, Medenwald says a huge chunk of their customer base has come from users just searching the Apple App Store. He says anytime a user searches in the Apple App Store for an in/out board, or digital in and out, their app immediately pops up.

"That gives us a giant chunk of customers," Medenwald says. "Because we are listed there and because we are listed for free, we get a lot of downloads."

Their work blogging and effectively using social media has also generated customers by giving a significant boost to the company website's Google rank. He says when they first started, their rank was abysmal, as any first-time developer's likely would be, but as they continued blogging and retweeting, that page rank went up. So much so that the Simply Made Apps website is the first result that pops up when someone uses Google—the largest search engine—to find a digital in/out board.

"Now we get a lot more traffic on the website courtesy of that, and this has helped us in a big, big way," he says.

Finally, Medenwald says a timely review also spiked interest in the app. As they were getting ready to release Simple In/Out, Medenwald says they began researching reviews of their competitors. Most of those reviews were of software for digital in/out boards that were outdated, so they compiled a list of all the writers that wrote those reviews. They sent each one an e-mail or a tweet letting them know about the Simple In/Out app in hopes they would be interested in writing about it.

(Continued on next page)

While most weren't interested in writing about their app, Medenwald says they did pique the interest of one *PC World* writer. He says that review really propelled the company in several ways.

"It was our first press," Medenwald says. "It wasn't long, probably only three or four paragraphs, but it was enough to drive a massive spike of traffic into our site. That helps for two big reasons: One, you have the chance to get new customers, but two, because of that link and traffic, our page rank in Google rose substantially. We went from page five or six all the way up to the bottom of the first page, all just based on a very popular link on a very popular site."

Knowing how important a good Google page rank is, Medenwald encourages first-time developers to focus on just getting information about the app and your company online. Facebook posts, tweets, blogs, as well as any press you garner, all boost your Google ranking. Medenwald says that although they haven't gotten any more big reviews, they have received numerous small mentions here and there, which, when added together, makes the effort worthwhile.

Medenwald also takes advantage of a free service called Help a Reporter Out (HARO), which links reporters throughout the United States with sources for the stories they are working on. Medenwald says he combs the daily queries from reporters looking for sources that he might be a match for. Some are app- and in/out board–related and some not. One story he remembers contributing to was about songs that entrepreneurs listen to.

"Songs. It has absolutely nothing to do with anything, but at the same time, because there is a link, and that link chases back to our site, it helps with our Google [rank]," Medenwald says. "If you keep plugging away and get your links here and there, eventually it adds up to good things."

Traditional and Online Media

Another popular way of drawing attention to your app is to generate media interest. The media has the potential to influence consumers in myriad ways. A good review could be the push a mobile device owner needs to download your app, while a bad review can leave a permanent stain on your app's reputation. That's why dealing with the media can be so unpredictable.

Unlike with your website and social media marketing, in which you have total control over the message, the media are in charge of what they want to say. Despite how functional and necessary you feel your app is, a writer—be it for a magazine, blog, or any other type of app-related outlet—may not feel the same way. Opening your app up to a professional review is a gamble. But if you are confident your app lives up to its billing, looks and works professionally, and is something others will want, it is a risk worth taking.

When trying to attract media attention, the specific aspects to focus on are who you're trying to appeal to and what you'll say if they want to listen. First off, you want to find the best types of reporters to contact. While those who write about and review mobile apps are an obvious target, they aren't the only writers you want to reach out to. You want to find anyone writing about the field your app fits into. If it is a photo app, you will want to find photography journalists; for a recipe app, you might reach out to writers who focus on food or grocery shopping.

This tactic also opens up a new audience of readers who aren't necessarily looking for a new app but are interested in the topic. You can't rely on customers who are solely searching for apps. To be successful, you will need to generate a customer base that's more than just app-centric. To get these more casual users, you need to target the things they are reading about—and for most, it isn't app-review sites.

Think long and hard about your target audience and its interests. Then you can determine what types of media those people are reading and how you can best tie in your app.

In the end, these types of outlets, more so than app reviewers, are where you will probably find the most success. Most first-time app developers agree that without some type of monetary enticement, the majority of app-review blogs and websites won't give you the time of day.

Developer Alex Genadinik says he found no success trying to get professional mobile app reviewers to write about his series of business start-up apps.

"I tried, but they basically all wanted to get paid, and the ones that were free had very small audiences, so it made no difference if they reviewed my app or not," he says.

While there is an abundance of app sites that want money in exchange for a review, there are plenty of others that take a more ethical approach to writing reviews. Dozens of sites are members of the Organization for App Testing Standards (OATS), whose goal is to improve the editorial ethics in the app-review industry. Their standards include rejecting all forms of paid reviews and clearly marking all advertisements as such.

It is best to work with these types of sites. While you might get a better "review" by paying for it, it won't do much for your credibility. Mobile device owners are savvy and can quickly sniff out reviews that don't seem authentic. Knowing you had to resort to a paid review doesn't always go over very well in the eyes of the reader.

Another easy market to target is your local community. Depending on the size of your city, an article in the local newspaper or magazine can really help to generate interest.

While the local media used to only comprise daily and weekly newspapers and a few television stations, the market is much larger today. The emergence of online journalism has opened a number of new local media doors. No longer should these outlets be viewed as any less significant, as the role of newspapers has diminished in the last decade. These hyper-local news sites (e.g., Patch.com) are now the places many people turn to first to learn about what is going on in their local communities.

As opposed to print newspapers and magazines, which are restricted in how many articles they can run in each edition, online sites have no such limitations. This means that the competition to get featured isn't as great.

Local communities often tend to support one of their own. So a short story or even a feature in any of the local outlets about you and your app could be all the motivation one of your neighbors needs to download the app. Once some members of the community start downloading and using the app, they may recommend it to others, which can only help with your download numbers.

While this might not help increase your customer base wildly, it is another area you don't want to neglect. In the end, you want to have as many irons in the marketing fire as you can, because you never know which one is going to pay off.

Media Messaging

Figuring out which media outlets to target is only a piece of the work required to garner media attention. The most important aspect is figuring out what to say and how to say it.

Journalists are busier than ever. Their time is limited, so knowing exactly how to appeal to them is essential, unless you want your attempt to get media attention to go nowhere. The most important thing to bring reporters is news that is going to be of true value to the majority of their readers.

Online Resources

If you are considering trying to get your app reviewed on a professional mobile app website, it is best to look for sites that are members of the Organization for App Testing Standards (OATS). Founded in 2009, the organization is designed to improve the ethical standards of many of these sites. All members refuse the increasingly popular practice of accepting money for a positive review. Here are the sites that have taken the OATS pledge. They'll decide whether or not to review your app based solely on its merit.

- AppAddict.net—http://appaddict.net
- AppFreak—http://AppFreakBlog.com
- AppGamer.net—http://appgamer.net
- AppModo—http://appmodo.com
- Appotography—http://Appotography.com
- Apps and Hats—http://appsandhats.com
- appSIZED—www.appsized.com
- AppSmile—www.appsmile.com
- AppStruck—http://appstruck.com
- Gamezbo—www.gamezebo.com
- iGame Radio—www.igameradio.com
- Insanely Great Mac—www.insanely-great.com
- iPad Insight—www.ipadinsight.com
- iPhoneCaptain—http://iPhoneCaptain.com
- iPhone Gamer Blog—www.iphonegamerblog.com
- iPhone Life magazine—http://iphonelife.com
- iPhone Reviews 2.0—http://ifonereviews.blogspot.com
- iSource—http://iSource.com
- iTito Themes Blog—http://ititothemes.wordpress.com
- iTracki—www.itracki.com
- Life in LoFi: iPhoneography—http://lifeinlofi.com
- Macworld Appguide—www.macworld.com/category/ios-apps
- No DPad—http://nodpad.com

Online Resources *(continued from page 143)*

- 148Apps—http://148Apps.com
- OneClickMac—www.oneclickmac.com
- RazorianFly—www.razorianfly.com
- SlapApp.com—http://slapapp.com
- Slide to Play—http://slidetoplay.com
- The Appera—http://theappera.com
- The App Goddess—www.theappgoddess.com
- The Canadian Reviewer—www.canadianreviewer.com
- The Portable Gamer—http://theportablegamer.com
- Today in iOS—http://tii.libsyn.com/
- TouchMyApps—http://touchmyapps.com
- TouchGen—http://touchgen.com

Simply stating that you have a new app for sale isn't going to make reporters—other than those who strictly cover apps—consider writing about you. They will delete your e-mail, and you and your app will quickly be forgotten.

While app reporters and reviewers will be interested in the technical aspects of the app and how it differs from what else is currently on the market, writers who cover different industries must be approached with a different set of details. For those writers, the information you provide needs to be of some service to their readers. This comes back to positioning yourself as an expert in the industries related to your app.

When approaching the media about their Home Inventory app, the Hamiltons say they take different approaches based on each outlet. When trying to drum up publicity for Home Inventory when there isn't anything new to announce, they tie the app in to something journalists are already covering.

In late summer and early fall, it was hurricanes. Diane Hamilton says she contacted newspapers up and down the East Coast with story ideas about how one way to prepare for a natural disaster is to have a detailed record of the valuables inside their homes, which is what their app does.

"We always try to associate [the app] with something relevant," Diane Hamilton says. "Home inventory is very relevant for hurricane season preparation. It is those kinds of things you want to highlight."

However, if they are trying to promote a new app's release or a new version of the app, Diane Hamilton says they take a more straightforward, technical approach.

"If we are contacting a technical publication, we want to reach out with some of the technical things the app can do better than anyone else in the market. If it is a new release, that is a whole different approach. You want people to try it so they talk about it as soon as it launched. So you want people who are willing to beta-test it or have a pre-look at it before launch day. It really depends on what the purpose of the [marketing] project is."

When trying to build relationships with influential app writers via online forums and blogs, Kevin Hamilton says it is important to become a participant in the conversation before trying to sell your app.

"Find online forums where your audience goes," Kevin Hamilton says. "Just become a participant. You don't want to be [selling] your software the whole time. Help people out. Participate in the conversation and get known. Then maybe mention that you have an app. If you provide a lot of useful help and information, then you can get the attention of the forum moderators and bloggers and the people who are actual tastemakers. But that takes a lot of time, and it isn't a strategy you can pull off in a week or two. If you have interest in the subject matter, you should be doing it anyway."

Once you have your messaging down, you need to determine how to contact each writer. The best way is to start with an e-mail. If you are writing about your app's new release, provide the most important and best functions of the app right off the bat. Remember, most reporters and writers get hundreds of e-mails each day.

To stick out from the crowd, you want to have an attention-grabbing subject line and a concise e-mail message that gets right to the point. In addition to the best features, you also want to make sure to tell the writer why this app is valuable to his or her readers, and what differentiates it from other apps out there. These e-mails should be no longer than a few paragraphs. Writers will quickly delete anything lengthier from their in-boxes.

In addition to what you put in the body of the e-mail, you should also include the link to your website and a press release. While many developers will agree that a press release on its own probably doesn't do much good, it does provide sufficient background about the app and about you for those journalists who decide to write about the app.

One of the first steps of most out-of-store marketing strategies is to reach out to the media and bloggers via a press release. While just sending a press release won't guarantee any coverage, it does send a message that you're serious and professional should a writer decide to pen a piece on you. Here are some releases that first-time developers Manne Darby and Peter Kruger wrote upon release of their first apps in February 2013. The samples, one longer and one shorter, provide excellent examples of the key messaging any new app press release should try to convey, including why someone needs the app, and what the app does.

SUCHEF RELEASE

What to Cook: SuChef Launches Website for Soon-to-Be-Released
Money- and Time-Saving Recipe App

BALTIMORE, MARYLAND, February 27, 2013—SuChef, LLC announced today the launch of its new website Su-Chef.com, in preparation for the upcoming launch of the innovative SuChef mobile recipe app for iPhone and Android. SuChef helps users save money and time on groceries, shopping, meal planning, and cooking by instantly searching the database of more than 100,000 recipes to find recipe options for ingredients already on hand.

Coming to iPhone and iPad in March, and Android devices shortly thereafter, the SuChef app allows users to speak, type, or barcode-scan their ingredients of choice into the smartphone or tablet for a recipe search that produces the best matches to determine what to cook from one day to the next. Users can tailor their results to practically any lifestyle, food preference, or dietary restrictions. Users can also search for recipes from a broad list of specific criteria without entering ingredients.

SuChef developer Manne Darby designed the app to help people make quick decisions about what to make for dinner using ingredients already in the pantry and fridge, saving unnecessary trips to the grocery store.

According to Darby, Americans log more than 60 million online searches for recipes each month.

"With that many searches and only a little over 100 million households, it becomes obvious that we frequently have no idea what to cook," Darby says. "Finding the right recipe through traditional online searches probably takes up more time than you think."

Data from the US Bureau of Labor Statistics reports that Americans spend on average almost fifty minutes each day, or a total of five and a half hours each week, grocery shopping, and that does not include the time spent just trying to decide what to cook. At a time when many people are trying to prepare more meals at home, the SuChef app simplifies everything from meal planning and grocery shopping to finding recipes that suit every taste and dietary need.

SuChef users can save more time by selecting the meals they would like to cook over any given time period and let the app create a grocery list based on those meals.

Most importantly, SuChef was designed to save money.

The average family wastes more than $1,000 per year on discarded groceries, according to studies by the Natural Resources Defense Council and other policy institutions and universities.

The leading cause of food waste is spoilage before the household has a chance to consume it. The second leading cause is food cooked in excessive amounts, leaving leftovers to be thrown away. Many people are guilty of buying large amounts of produce at once, only for much of it to go bad before it's eaten. The same problem is typical with meat, eggs, milk, and other foods that have limited shelf lives or expiration dates.

SuChef users can save $50 or more each month on groceries by delivering recipes specifically selected to use the food that has already been bought. The app can create a grocery list from preselected recipes to avoid purchasing unnecessary groceries, which can add up to significant savings on the overall grocery bill.

The Su-Chef.com website offers in-depth information on the SuChef app, plus a regularly updated blog with tips and information on food-related topics.

When the SuChef app becomes available in March, it can be downloaded from the Apple App Store to iPhone and iPad.

For more information on the SuChef website or app, visit www.Su-Chef.com.

ROCK LOBBY RELEASE

Rock Lobby Is Now Available in the Apple App Store

NEW YORK, February 26, 2013—Rock Lobby, the first mobile application designed to power local live music discovery with real-time fan-based reviews, is now available for iOS. With a simple design and easy-to-use interface, Rock Lobby enables concertgoers to rate live music, write reviews, and upload photos directly from their mobile device. In addition, Rock Lobby gives fans the ability to discover the best live music nearby by connecting them to reviews from an informed community of music-loving people in their area.

There are plenty of apps that help people find shows and even allow fans to post photos or comments regarding a show they attend, but Rock Lobby sets itself apart by empowering the fans to become the critics. Simplicity is essential when trying to upload photos and write reviews from a live concert, so Rock Lobby utilizes a straightforward and easy-to-use design. Rock Lobby was built as a native application for iOS leading to a fast, fluid, and smooth user experience.

Features:

- Rate and write reviews for live music
- Search through an extensive list of upcoming shows
- View a map with information and ratings for the best upcoming and current shows in your area, updated in real time
- Read reviews by an informed community of music-loving people
- Follow your friends, fellow music fans, your favorite bands or venues to keep track of what you care about
- Find and follow specific shows, fans, artists, and venues

"The days of people looking primarily to Rolling Stone, NPR, and MTV for new music are long over," says Peter Kruger, CEO of Rock Lobby. "We want to help music fans find great local music, and we want to empower the critic inside each fan. The 'Rock Star' will no longer be dictated or manufactured by the industry, but instead will be discovered organically by a community of informed fans."

For more information, visit rocklobby.com.

Things you want to make sure to include in your press release include:

- An attention-grabbing headline
- All the facts on your app: what it is, key features, and how it benefits users
- Quotes from you explaining the app and putting into context why someone would want to download it
- Details on where the app can be downloaded, and for how much
- Contact information so reporters with additional questions can easily reach you

Once you send your initial e-mail to a reporter or blogger, you want to give that person time to respond. The majority of writers are not going to respond immediately with a yes or no.

If you don't hear anything within a week, follow up. Reporters are busy, so there is a chance your e-mail was overlooked, or they just haven't had time to respond. A follow-up, preferably by phone, should help spur them on.

If a reporter is interested in writing about you, your strategy is working and you need to replicate it with other outlets. If a reporter says no, dig for some more information about why. Find out if there is someone at the publication who would be a better fit to write about your app, or inquire why, if that reporter is the best person, the story wasn't appealing.

By hearing why reporters or bloggers are saying no, you will be better able to tailor your message in the future. With all forms of PR, there is a lot of trial and error, and this aspect is no exception.

In the end, getting media coverage of any kind is about bringing some value to the table. Often, it isn't just going to be that you have a new app to sell. Always be working to tie your app in to something relevant that is going on. You are going to be much more successful in getting the media's attention by figuring out a way to include yourself and your app into a conversation they're already having.

Marketing to the App Stores

Another valuable way to increase your visibility is by drawing the attention of the app stores. Each week, the app stores highlight and feature the apps they feel are worth downloading. These feature and editor selections carry a lot of weight with mobile device users. Earning such recognition can go a long way toward your app's success.

The hard part with this approach is that this can only be done indirectly. While you can easily send out a press release or try a few tweets to get ahold of a writer or journalist, you don't have that same ease with app stores. Instead of contacting them directly, you will need to start thinking like them in order to get their attention.

Kevin Hamilton says the main marketing strategy of his Richmond-based company, Binary Formations, is to get recognized by Apple in the Apple App Store.

"We have one effective marketing strategy, and we call it Apple love," Kevin Hamilton says. "What it is, is essentially getting the attention of Apple."

While the Hamiltons originally built Home Inventory as an application for Mac computers, they eventually decided to build a mobile app version that would work in tandem with their Mac app. At the time, Kevin Hamilton says there was a vast number of apps that worked in partnership with other computer or web-based apps, but they all worked in the same way. He says the mobile versions all tended to just be a replica of the computer or web-based versions.

To catch Apple's eye, Kevin Hamilton says they built their mobile version to work more as an extended feature of their app. Instead of just using the mobile app to sync up with their Mac version, the Hamiltons created their app so mobile users could connect via Wi-Fi to their Mac application, allowing them to go around their house and take actual photos of each item being inventoried.

"We wanted to use the iPhone in conjunction with the Mac in a different way than what most people did," Kevin Hamilton says. "That got Apple's attention, and they featured us very heavily in the [Apple] App Store. And that, quite frankly, made the difference between doing this as a hobby and doing this as a real business."

To get that Apple attention, Kevin Hamilton says it was important to think like the computer giant throughout the app's development by building the app with the features and new technology Apple is most focused on.

When building the latest version of their app, Home Inventory 3, the Hamiltons used some of Apple's newer technologies, like retina graphics and supported full-screen mode.

"That is one common theme you will hear again and again: If you want to get Apple's attention, you want to look at the technologies they are either currently promoting, or, if you are looking at beta versions, the things you know they are going to promote, and target them. Because Apple always does little sub-features of key apps that target those [technologies]. In this case, it worked out really well, because ultimately we ended up being chosen as editor's choice.

"We always say we have two audiences we write for: One audience is the customer, of course—they are our primary audience. But you always keep the Apple Store in mind. There are only a limited number of featured spots, and you want them. It is a huge, huge, huge deal to get some type of feature. That is the kind of marketing we have been most effective at."

Kevin Hamilton says the increase in downloads they received after getting featured by Apple was massive. He estimates the extra attention from Apple brought in more than ten times the number of downloads they would have gotten without the in-store publicity.

Paid PR

If you aren't able to generate publicity for free, you always have the option to pay for some. There are plenty of paid options for PR help, from high-priced public relations firms to Google or Facebook ads. Paid marketing strategies include:

- Public relations firms: Whether it is a big-city firm or a small boutique operation, public relations firms are charged with handling all aspects of PR. Finding target audiences, crafting messages, writing press releases, and contacting and enticing reporters to write about your app are all responsibilities a quality PR firm can handle. While this option may provide all of the services you desire, it is also the most costly, so it is important to weigh what kind of return you feel you can get on that investment.

- Pay-per-click advertising: This is a form of online advertising in which you only pay the ad's publisher, typically a website owner, when someone clicks on the ad. This is a much cheaper form of paid PR. Research shows that the advertiser—who would be you, in this case—pays less than 90 cents per click.

- E-mail marketing: E-mail marketing generates consumer interest by sending out targeted e-mails about your app. This can be done in various ways, including via newsletters, promotional campaigns, and surveys. The benefit of e-mail marketing, as opposed to direct mail, is that there are built-in tools that allow you to see who is opening the e-mails to better determine your target audience. There are a number of online e-mail marketing services that can set you up with everything you need to launch a campaign. These cost anywhere from $7 to $15, to send e-mails to as many as 500 consumers, to as much as $90 to $300, to send out up to 25,000 e-mails.

- Social network advertising: While you can always promote your business or app for free on Facebook, Twitter, and the other social networks, there are paid advertising opportunities on each site, as well. These are the ads that are folded into news and Twitter feeds. With this strategy, you usually have the option of paying either by click or by impression.

- Conventions and conferences: One of the best ways to get your app noticed by those in the industry is to attend conferences and conventions in industries related to your app. For example, shortly after launching his Rock Lobby app, New York City developer Peter Kruger attended the South By Southwest (SXSW) festival in Texas. Geared toward music and technology lovers, the conference proved to be a perfect place for Kruger to meet people in the music industry and sell them on the beauty of his app. He says the added expense paid off when he was able to partner up with a concert ticket vendor, who helped find new and profitable ways to monetize his app.

For those wanting to invest in some paid PR, Kevin Hamilton advises that before diving in, you really make sure it will help to make you money in the end.

"Low-dollar PR is probably going to be very ineffective, and high-dollar PR, when you are talking about apps—particularly some that sell for only a couple of dollars each—needs to have a ridiculous return to even break even," Hamilton says. "For most apps, a really effective PR person doesn't make sense."

Chapter Recap

One of the most difficult yet integral aspects of launching a new app is generating publicity for it outside of the app store. If mobile device owners don't know it exists, the likelihood that they will ever download it is slim. To effectively promote your app, your business, and yourself, you need to employ a variety of marketing strategies:

- Build a website: Your website will serve as your app's online home. With this website, you have the chance to teach potential customers more about your app, as well as show them where they can buy it. The website must include all the facts about your app, high-quality screenshots, direct links to your product pages inside the app stores, and a way to contact you. Other aspects to consider include adding a blog to help boost SEO, and a newsroom page where the press can find all your press releases and media kits.

- Social networking: Using social media, including Facebook, Twitter, Google+, etc., is an excellent way for you to generate some free attention for your app. Once you are signed up with each social network, you need to start collecting fans and followers. It is especially important to try and make connections with those who have the most influence on your target audience, such as bloggers and app experts.

- Traditional and online media: While there are a variety of outlets you can contact, this can be one of the most difficult parts of opening a home-based app development business. You need to approach not only app outlets, but also those related to your industry and in your hometown. When contacting the media, be sure to position your message in such a way that it doesn't seem like all you have is an app for sale. Always try to tie your app in with something relevant and already being talked about in the news.

- App-store targeting: Getting recognized in the app stores as an app worth downloading can bring an immense amount of traffic your way. To attract the app stores' attention, you can focus on building your app using the technology the stores are trying to promote most. While there are no guarantees with this method, if it works, the dividends will be massive.

- Paid advertising: If you have some money to spend, you might want to consider investing in some paid marketing. There are a variety of options, from pay-per-click ads to PR firms, depending on how much you want to spend.

13 | Running Your Business

Now that you are selling your app and have a marketing plan in place that will get it some attention, you need to spend time focusing on running your business, both professionally and financially.

From a professional standpoint, it is critical to make sure you continue to keep busy now that the development has come to an end. Unless you are jumping right back into developing a second app, you are going to work on structuring your time differently.

From a financial perspective, it is important to start brushing up on your accounting skills to ensure that you know what you are doing when money from your first app starts rolling in.

Day-to-Day Operations

Up until now, you have been totally focused on getting your first app built and marketed. More than likely, you have had very little downtime. That feeling of constantly being on the go, however, is likely going to dwindle quickly.

While it would be nice to just sit back, rest, and watch your money roll in, successful businesses aren't built that way. Of course, you should take some time to relax and celebrate; you've just finished a monumental task that we hope is the start of something really successful. However, once you have taken time to recharge, you need to get moving again. Profitable businesses are always working, and those who run them always have an eye on what's next.

What's next in this case is both careful tracking of who is downloading your app, and how much money is coming in. Now that your app is finally being sold, you can really start to get a feel for who your customers are and how much they are willing to spend for your product. With each download, you gain a little more insight into exactly who your target audience is. Once you start to build up some substantial data, you will want to see how you can better position your app with not only your in-store marketing, but also how you are trying to target customers outside of the app stores.

You also want to keep a close eye on your competitors. How have their downloads changed since you entered the marketplace? Have you been able to creep into their customer base, or are they still keeping a strong grip on things? Either way, this gives you information on the type of features and functionality your customers want.

If you have taken over the market share, you are on the right track. If not, your competitors are still offering a product that is better than yours, or, at the very least, marketed better than yours. If that's the case, you need to go back and figure out what update you can make to your app to make it more appealing to consumers, or find a way to make more mobile device owners aware of it.

App Updates

Another area you will be focused on after the release of your app is fixing any new bugs that your customers find. Despite all the work you put into testing the app before releasing it, there will inevitably be flaws that you never anticipated.

While you could choose to leave the errors alone and let the chips fall where they may, you would be taking a huge risk. If a bug is found and no update is provided within a reasonable amount of time, your customers may get angry. All they want is for your app to do what you said it was going to do; when you don't deliver on that, they are going to fight back with the only weapon they have: a negative review.

Getting too many bad reviews complaining about bugs and errors that have never been fixed will cause potential customers to think twice about downloading your app. Why would they waste their money on an app that will keep crashing?

You would be wise to take your customers' feedback seriously. When they point out errors, it is up to you to fix them. If you programmed the app yourself, you need to go back into the coding and fix what's broken. If you worked with a programmer, you need to contact that person again to see how quickly he or she can resolve the issue.

In most cases, outside programmers work with developers updating the app for only a certain amount of time after its release. That's why you really should contact your programmer as soon as customers alert you to any problems they are having.

In addition to working on making sure the current app is living up to expectations, you can start to prepare for your next mobile app. It is never too early to start conducting some more research on where a new idea fits in.

Expert's View: The Challenges of Solopreneurship

Jeff Hellenbrand

Business coach Jeff Hellenbrand says that running any business is hard enough, but operating a home-based business as a solopreneur comes with its own unique challenges.

One of the first is staying motivated each day without a boss or coworker breathing down your back. Hellenbrand, a home-based business owner and founder of Cake Coaching, which specializes in giving wedding planners the tools they need to succeed, says it can be especially tough staying driven once that so-called "honeymoon" phase of running your own business wears off.

"We get really psyched up, and then it just kind of fades," Hellenbrand says. "Whenever that ends, whether it's six weeks or six months later, it's like 'Oh, crap, how do I keep this up?' "

Hellenbrand says that one of the key parts of being able to stay motivated each day comes through having a serious passion about what you're doing.

"Waking up with that in mind every day is huge," Hellenbrand says. "The second thing that goes with that is knowing how each little thing fits into that big picture. A lot of people get sidetracked when they are working on that little piece of the puzzle and they don't make that connection. [They need] to approach this from a mindful perspective—that I am doing this very detailed work because this is going to help me get funding, or this is to help the core part of the app. Just making that connection really helps."

When it comes to working day-to-day, Hellenbrand says it is important to set some sort of schedule. Because everyone is different, Hellenbrand says developers need to set a schedule that works best for them.

For some, that may mean a traditional nine-to-five schedule, while for others it might mean working four hours in the morning and five hours at night. While making sure you get work done is vital, Hellenbrand says it is also important to be able to take advantage of the benefits of running your own business from home.

"How do you work best?" Hellenbrand asks. "You need to figure out when you are the most energized and when the best times are for you to work, and that is different for

(Continued on next page)

everyone. Knowing yourself is really the key. But, if you don't think about it mindfully, you just 'half work' all of the time, and that is the danger of not setting boundaries."

No matter what kind of schedule you set, Hellenbrand says it is important that home-based business owners not beat themselves up when they don't get as much accomplished as they wanted.

"The key with not letting a bad day or bad week turn into a bad year is all about guilt," he says. "As entrepreneurs, we really tend to beat ourselves up for what we didn't do. It comes down to expectations. Most of the entrepreneurs I work with have expectations that are completely out of whack. We have this crazy idea of what we can get done in any given time period, which is just nowhere near true. I think that tends to lead to us feeling unproductive, even if we had a really productive week. I think the best thing you can do is just get rid of those expectations as much as possible. Don't spend a lot of time rehashing the past. The only moment we have is this one, and if we spend it regretting the past, it isn't the best use of your time. In that moment it is about dropping the guilt and recognizing that feeling guilty isn't helpful, so we can make a different choice."

Another challenge that home-based business owners often face is isolation. Working from home by yourself can be a lonely venture. Hellenbrand says that until you actually do start working by yourself, you won't realize how much those little interactions around the office truly mattered.

"The key is to listen to yourself," Hellenbrand says. "Do you like chatting with people for a few minutes? Would you rather connect with a good friend for a couple hours once a week? Know what you need and get it on the calendar. Because you're scheduling something with another person, you're much more likely to do it."

Hellenbrand believes it comes down to entrepreneurs looking inside themselves to figure out how they can work best, and to determine the motivational tactics that will help them get there.

Regardless of what the task is, you must be working on something every day. Don't let the freedom that working from home affords be a negative. For your business to succeed, it needs careful, daily attention. Letting yourself get distracted or unmotivated is the quickest way to find your business closed up and yourself looking for work again in the ultracompetitive job market.

Financial Bookkeeping

Besides focusing on running your business from an operational standpoint, you need to make sure you are taking care of things on the financial end. Proper tracking of expenses and revenues is integral to the success of any profitable business.

How can you accurately say your business is a winner if you don't know exactly how much money you're making or losing? Besides giving you an accurate picture of where your business stands, there are a number of other benefits to keeping proper financial records.

According to the IRS, maintaining good records also helps with preparing important and official financial statements, which include both income statements and a balance sheet, keeping track of deductible expenses, and preparing your tax returns.

How to Keep Financial Records

For the most part, there are only two numbers you really need to track: revenue and expenses. You want to know exactly how much money you are spending each month and year versus how much you are bringing in. If you are taking in more than you are spending, your business is moving in the right direction. If expenses are higher than revenue, you need to quickly figure out how to turn those numbers around. Your business won't last very long if you spend more than you make each month.

There are a variety of ways to track this information. Options include writing everything down on paper or using state-of-the-art financial software.

Before getting started, you should evaluate each option to see which one will be right for you. For example, while writing things down might seem easiest, it can cause more headaches than you might expect. A computer isn't involved, so it is up to you to make each calculation correctly. Make one math mistake and your company's financial picture could be totally shot.

On the other hand, while financial accounting software makes every calculation correctly, it comes at a high cost. The top-rated accounting software options can run anywhere from $80 to $1,800, depending on the version you select. So while the software will make things more convenient, you have to determine if it fits into your budget.

Texas business coach Mike O'Neal, who developed his own software program for financial recordkeeping, says what really matters in the end is that you are doing it. Without proper recordkeeping, he says, there is no way a business can operate efficiently.

"I don't care how you track it, as long as you use something," O'Neal says, referring to either electronic or paper options. "Because once you keep track of those things—your multiple streams of income, your networking breakfast, your office supplies, your legal costs, virtual assistants, advertising, business trips, credit card costs—now you can become more efficient because you can start asking questions."

For example, O'Neal says a new business owner may attend networking meetings, at a cost of $400 a month, to drum up some new customers and clients. By knowing exactly how much you're spending on those meetings each month, O'Neal says you can then go back and determine if you are getting $400 worth of new business out of them. If so, he advises continuing to go. If not, then you may want to consider putting that money into something else that might make more of a difference.

"Unless you have that information, though, you can't even ask those questions," he says. "So it's not keeping track of the dollars and pennies—that's not the important stuff. The important part is, now that you have that information, you can modify your business to be much more efficient."

Regardless of which option you choose, the fundamentals of how you actually keep financial records are the same. Each time you spend money on the business, whether it's on a bill or on new equipment, you need to write it down or enter it into your software. For each expense, note whom you paid the money to, the date you paid it, and exactly how much you spent.

For revenue, the same is true. Each time you make a sale or receive a check, you need to write that down or input it into your software as well. Similarly, you must make note of where the money came from, when you received it, and how much you got.

At first, all you will have are expenses. It is going to cost money to launch your business, register as a developer, build your app, and market it. These are all expenses you will be making before you ever see a dime come rolling in.

You won't start seeing any revenue until your app hits the app stores. Don't, however, expect to get paid each time a mobile device owner downloads your app or makes an in-app purchase. Instead, the app stores all pay developers once a month for the money they've earned over the past thirty days. So, until you are selling multiple apps, you can expect to only get paid once a month from each of the stores. This will make keeping financial records pretty easy initially.

However, as you move on to developing your second and third apps, more revenue and expenditure streams will start flowing, making the process substantially more complicated.

Once your business becomes more advanced, there are additional financial records you will want to keep. These include a profit and loss statement, a cash flow statement, and a balance sheet. When put together, these financial statements provide a complete picture of a business's financial health and future. At this point, you may want to consider hiring a financial bookkeeper who will track these things for you.

Now that you have moved beyond the initial development stage into running the day-to-day operations, it is time to think about moving back again.

Chapter Recap

After months of spending all your time focused on getting your app built, it can be a big transition when the development phase stops. Even though you may not be working on creating new apps, you still need to make sure you are keeping your business running and moving forward. Here is a rundown of the tasks you should be working on when not spending time actually developing your app:

■ App monitoring: Now that you have an app in the market, you want to track how it is doing and how it's affecting your competitors. Each day, track downloads of your app and compare against those of your competitors. Are you taking a chunk out of their market share, or is your app falling by the wayside? Having this information can help you to tweak your app to ensure that it is what consumers want.

■ Gather feedback: You need to listen closely to what your customers are saying about your app. Which features do they like, and which ones don't they like? When they alert you to a problem, take it seriously. Not solving their problems could incite negative reviews, which can tank your app sales.

■ Update your app: When you learn of bugs that are negatively affecting your app, you need to fix them. The success of your app depends on how well you respond. If you programmed the app on your own, fix these bugs as quickly as possible. If you hired a freelancer or digital agency to program your app, work with them to correct the problems.

■ Keep detailed financial records: To be a profitable and successful business, you need to know how much money you are making. The only way to know if you're making money is to track all expenses and revenue carefully. It doesn't matter whether you use paper and pencil or a sophisticated computer program, as long as you are tracking what's going out versus what's coming in.

Business Endgame

Now that you have developed your first app, placed it in the marketplace, and spent time running the business while not in the development phase, it is time to decide if you want to do it all over again.

A successful business isn't going to be built off just one app. To grow your business, you need to expand on your app offerings. To do so means going through the entire development stage all over again. You must complete the research, programming, and marketing every time you want to launch a new app.

So now is the time to reflect on your experience. Was it as fun as you hoped? Was it harder than you expected? What were the challenges you faced the last time, and how, if possible, will you avoid them moving forward?

Another contributing factor will be the success of your first app. Is your app generating the downloads you expected? Are you making back the money you invested?

Shutting Down

If you didn't enjoy the development experience and your app isn't generating the consumer interest you were hoping for, you'll want to consider closing up shop. It doesn't make much sense to continue trying to run a business that you aren't enjoying and have dwindling passion for.

There is nothing wrong with stepping away. In fact, a 2013 study by researchers at Oregon State and Utah State universities revealed that the best entrepreneurs are those who know how to best balance when to risk opening a new business with when to walk away from a venture because things are heading south.

Don't feel the need to hang on to the business because of what you've invested. Since you are working from home and don't have employees to worry about, there won't be many financial consequences to shutting your business down. You don't have office rent to pay, and you won't have to worry about firing any staff members. In the end, you have really only invested money in building and marketing your app, not in the structure of the business.

What doesn't make sense is to keep operating a business that isn't enjoyable and isn't making any money. It's not worth the financial risk to invest money into the building and marketing of a second app in the hopes that you will change your opinion on working in the mobile app industry.

But if you enjoyed the process, regardless of whether or not your first app is making any money, then you will want to think about making another one.

Growing Your Business

While ideally your first app is making money, you can't base your decision to develop more apps on just that alone. The key is whether or not you enjoyed developing the app, researching the marketplace, and launching your marketing campaign.

If you enjoyed the experience and have become even more passionate about it than you were before you started, it's worth considering moving forward, regardless of how successful that first app was. You will be surprised at how much you learned when making the first one, and how much you will improve the second time around. Your improvement will only lead to a better app, from concept to design to functionality.

To grow the business, you need to start the development process over from the start. First item is coming up with a new idea. Many developers like to stick to one genre when developing apps, while others aren't afraid to jump all over the place. Regardless, it is all about researching the idea to make sure it will be successful.

If you are sticking with the same type of app, you should already have a handle on the market and competitors. However, you still need to determine how your new app will fit within the market, and top what's already out there. Also, you need to make sure it is different enough from your first app that consumers would want to buy both, and not just one or the other.

If you aren't sticking to the same genre, you have to start your research over from scratch. That means determining how your new app will fit into the marketplace and what competitors already exist. This is the exact same process you went through with your first app; the only difference is that you should have a much better idea of what you should be looking for this time around.

It is important to learn from your mistakes in order to make your development process more efficient. That starts with the research. Don't waste time studying things that aren't going to help you. Zero in on the information you need—who your competitors are, what their apps can do, what kind of sales they have, and how you can steal their share of the marketplace—so you can move on to designing the app.

Programming the app should be easier the second time around, as well, both for developers who did it themselves and those who outsourced to a professional coder. If you programmed the app yourself, you know exactly how the operating system and developer tools function. You won't need to spend that time getting up to speed on how everything works. Instead, you can jump right into the programming, which will most likely speed up your development time considerably.

If you hired an outsider to program your app, you can save time by hiring that person or agency again. If you had a good working relationship with the programmer and liked the work they produced, give them another go.

Even if you didn't like them and want to hire someone else, the process won't be as difficult and time-consuming as it was the first time around. This time, you know what type of programmer you are looking for and what working style meshes best with yours. Knowing that beforehand makes finding someone compatible to work with much easier.

The only part of the development process that probably won't get any easier, no matter how many apps you produce, is the marketing aspect. The same exhaustive amount of work is needed each time you release an app. Even though you might have better contacts and sources as your business becomes more established, you still have to work with them and entice them into writing what you want.

With marketing there are never any guarantees. What works for one app might not play as well with another. Each time you release a new app, you will have to put in the same amount of effort, if not more, to get the publicity you're after.

Money

Even though money shouldn't be the deciding factor when it comes to the decision to move your business forward, it usually will play a part in your decision. Growing your business will cost money, and you need to determine whether you have enough to do what you want and, if not, where you will get it from.

Hopefully, your first app is drawing consumer interest, and you are on your way to at least making your money back, if not profiting. If this is the case, getting the money to fund your second development likely won't be as much of a problem.

You can use the revenue you have coming in to program and market a second app. Ideally, the sales from your first app will totally support the development of your second app, and you won't have to put any additional money into the business.

However, if your app isn't generating enough money to build a second app, or isn't generating any revenue at all, you will need to find another source of funding. Just like when you started, you can find the money from a variety of sources. Whether it's friends and family, a bank, or crowdfunding (a way to raise money online from other individuals or companies), there are a number of options available to entrepreneurs in need of funding.

You may run into a problem if you have already been to these sources once for money. The fact that you weren't able to turn a profit with the last loan they gave you won't give them much faith in your ability to do it this time around. If you do end up going to the same source for funding, it will be critical that you provide them with a detailed plan on how this app is different, and why it will be profitable this time.

Down the Road

With each app you develop, the process is going to get easier. Everything will become more efficient, which should cut down on development, as well as the time you spend between development periods.

You should get to a point where you are developing multiple apps at one time, and where you can start programming a new app as soon as you are marketing another, and not waste time waiting for results. This will help to grow your business at a more rapid pace and provide additional streams of income.

If you are trying to take your business to that next level, you will eventually want to start growing in ways other than just by adding more apps. Once you see that you have a knack for coming up with good ideas that consumers will spend money on, you can start to grow your business's footprint.

While you started off as a one-person show, to really expand your business you will need more manpower. Eventually you will want to add employees who can complement your skills. This may mean a professional programmer if you aren't experienced enough, or a marketing specialist trained to drum up publicity for small businesses.

In time, as you add more employees, your business might outgrow the confines of your home. When that occurs, you will need to find the right type of working environment that encourages collaboration and provides you room to grow in the future.

With employees and office space come a whole new set of expenses and legal rules that need to be followed, so it is important to make sure you are truly ready for those steps before actually taking them.

It is critical to have proper expectations about this. You might not reach this stage for five years, ten years, or maybe ever. And that's okay. There is nothing wrong with keeping your business small, as long as you are okay with the results you get from it.

The smaller you are, the less revenue you can expect to bring in. The larger your business gets and the more apps you have in the marketplace, the greater chance you have of bringing in more money.

In the end, growing your business comes down to you and how much you are willing to invest. It took a tremendous amount of energy to launch your business and develop your first app. To grow it, it's going to take even more. If you are ready for the challenge, I encourage you to take that leap and keep pushing forward.

Chapter Recap

Growing your business is dependent on whether or not you want to keep developing apps. To do so, you want to have an even greater drive and determination than you did the first go-round. Here are four key questions you need to be asking before you decide to move forward with expanding your business and app offerings:

1. Did you enjoy the development process?

This is the first and most important process. If you didn't like the research or working with the programmer or the effort it took to market it, you should probably consider moving in a direction that doesn't involve developing apps. However, if you had fun developing your app, and your passion for the industry intensified during the process, it's worth exploring whether you have the ideas and resources to grow your business.

2. Do you have ideas for other apps?

To expand your business, you will need more ideas for apps that are going to resonate with consumers. These can either be in the same genre as the first app, or completely different. All that matters is that you spend the necessary time researching the idea to determine if it can be successful.

3. Do you have enough money to grow your business?

While money should not be the sole factor in whether or not you decide to grow your business, it definitely must be considered. To develop more apps and expand your company, you are going to need more money. If your first app was successful, you should have enough revenue coming in to develop a second app. If your app isn't getting many downloads, you need to figure out a funding source. To grow your business, you will need more money, so be sure you have enough moving forward.

4. Are you ready to expand outside the home?

As you become more efficient with the development process and are able to start developing multiple apps at one time, you will need to consider expanding beyond just new apps. At some point, your growing business may need employees and office space. Don't rush to get to this point, however. Make sure you are as skilled and proficient as you can be with the development process before trying to take your business to that next level. Being on that next level comes with a massive amount of expense and legal risk.

Appendix A: Glossary

Ad impressions: The number of times an advertisement inside a mobile app is displayed or clicked on.

Android: A mobile operating system that runs on Java. Android apps are sold in the Google Play Store, the Amazon Appstore, and a variety of other online app marketplaces.

Android SDK: The development kit that provides developers with the tools needed to build an Android-powered mobile app.

Apple App Store: The online home for all mobile apps for Apple devices. This is the only legal marketplace through which Apple device owners can purchase iOS apps.

Application: A software program designed to perform a specific function. Apps can run on mobile devices, personal computers, and online.

App stores: Online marketplaces where mobile device owners can purchase mobile apps. The three most popular app stores are the Apple App Store, the Google Play Store, and the Amazon Appstore.

Beta testing: The process of having outsiders play around with an app to make sure it doesn't have any obvious bugs or other defects.

Digital agency: A professional firm with a team of specialists that is able to work on every aspect of a mobile app, from design and user interface to programming and connectivity. Such services can cost anywhere from $25,000 to $100,000.

Do-it-yourself service: An online service that gives developers with no programming experience the opportunity to quickly and easily build a functioning app.

Domain name: A website's online address. A domain name must be officially registered before it can be used online.

E-mail marketing: A strategy for boosting consumer interest by sending targeted e-mails that promote a product or, specifically, an app. The e-mails can include newsletters, promotional campaigns, or surveys about the product.

Freelancer: Professionals with specific skills, including mobile application programming, who can be hired on a per-project basis.

Google Play: Currently, the most popular Android app marketplace. As of July 2013, there were more than one million apps in the Google Play app store.

Icon: An app's logo of sorts. This image is shown on the app's product page, and can be seen on a mobile device after it has been installed.

In-app advertising: Advertisements that appear after a user opens the app. These ads are commonly used by developers to make money off an app that they let consumers download for free.

In-app purchasing: Purchases made by consumers while using the app. This is a monetary strategy for developers trying to make money off their mobile app.

iOS: The Apple operating system. All Apple apps for the iPhone, iPad, and iPod are run on this operating system.

Java: The primary Android programming language that developers must use when designing Android apps.

Keywords: The words assigned to an app by the developer that help the app marketplaces determine which apps pop up when certain terms are searched.

Limited liability company: A type of business structure that combines the benefits of a partnership and corporation by giving owners personal liability protection and special tax breaks.

Mobile app: An application that is designed specifically to work on a mobile device, such as a smartphone or tablet.

Nondisclosure agreement: A legal document that protects the parties that sign it from having their ideas stolen. For mobile developers, they are used when working with a freelancer or digital agency.

Objective-C: The programming code Apple requires all developers to use when designing apps for their products on the iOS system.

Paid downloads: A strategy that mobile developers use to make money off their mobile app. This entails charging customers a set fee up front for use of the app.

Pay-per-click advertising: A form of online advertising in which the advertiser only pays the ad's publisher, typically a website owner, when someone clicks on the ad. This is a common form of mobile app marketing.

Product description: The app's page inside each app store. This provides an opportunity for the seller to give consumers more details about their app. It includes a written description and screenshots of the app.

Programmer: A computer professional who specializes in building software. They have the skills needed to code the software, which in this case is the mobile app.

S Corporation: A type of business structure that gives companies the limited liability benefits of being a corporation with the tax advantages that come with being a partnership or LLC.

Screenshots: Pictures of what the app looks like while in use. Screenshots are used to give consumers a better idea of what to expect from the app after downloading it.

Search engine optimization (SEO): A strategy used by Google, Yahoo, and the other search engines to determine the results that pop up each time a visitor makes a search on the site. The better a company's SEO, the higher its website will pop up in the search results.

Service agreement contract: A legal contract that spells out the details of a job and what's expected. It includes the agreed-upon price, project timeline, terms for termination, and payment details.

Social network advertising: Paid advertising opportunities offered by popular social networking sites such as Facebook and Twitter.

Sole proprietorship: A type of business structure that provides the least amount of legal protection. The business is not taxed separately. Any income and expenses are reported on the standard IRS Form 1040.

Updates: Changes made to the app following its release. Once developers learn of problems and come up with ways to improve the app, they can release an update that becomes available to all current and future customers.

Xcode: Apple's developer environment that provides users with a workspace and the tools needed to build and program a functioning mobile app for the iPhone, iPad, or Mac computer.

Business Plan Templates

These sites offer entrepreneurs sample business plans and templates to help them write their own. They provide an excellent outline of the items that should be included in your business plan.

- Bplans: www.bplans.com/sample_business_plans.php#.UhQbcLyE4kc

- Entrepreneur: www.entrepreneur.com/landing/216013

- Microsoft: http://office.microsoft.com/en-us/templates/business-plan-for-startup-business-TC001017520.aspx

- SCORE: www.score.org/resources/business-plans-financial-statements-template-gallery

- US Small Business Administration: www.sba.gov/business-plan/1

- vFinance, Inc.: www.vfinance.com/invisiframe.asp?URL=%2Fhome.asp%3FToolPage%3Dbizplan_download.asp%26bps%3D1%26invisiframe%3D1

Researching the Competition

The best way to determine how your app should look and act is to research what the competition is offering. These online sites provide app store search engines so you can get a full picture of the competitors in your space.

- Appolicious: www.appolicious.com

- uQuery: http://uquery.com

Registering as a Developer

- Amazon: https://developer.amazon.com/welcome.html

- Android: http://developer.android.com/tools/index.html

- Apple: https://developer.apple.com/register/index.action

- Google Play: https://play.google.com/apps/publish/v2/signup

Apple Programming Tutorials

These online tutorials offer programmers tips and tricks for ensuring that their iOS app performs and looks as expected. Tutorials include everything from the basics on Objective-C to developing an app for international sales.

- Write Objective-C Code: Helps users become acquainted with Apple's primary programming language. https://developer.apple.com/library/ios/#referencelibrary/GettingStarted/RoadMapiOS/chapters/WriteObjective-CCode/WriteObjective-CCode/WriteObjective-CCode.html

- Acquire Foundational Programming Skills: This is the foundation toolkit for all iOS programming. https://developer.apple.com/library/ios/#referencelibrary/GettingStarted/RoadMapiOS/chapters/AcquireBasicProgrammingSkills/AcquireBasicSkills/AcquireBasicSkills.html

- Survey the Major Frameworks: A rundown of the frameworks most commonly used by iOS developers. https://developer.apple.com/library/ios/#referencelibrary/GettingStarted/RoadMapiOS/chapters/SurveytheMajorFrameworks/SurveytheMajorFrameworks/SurveytheMajorFrameworks.html

- Frameworks: This describes the kinds of methods found in Objective-C frameworks and explains how you can integrate your app's code with a framework's code. https://developer.apple.com/library/ios/#referencelibrary/GettingStarted/RoadMapiOS/chapters/Frameworks.html

- Streamline Your App with Design Patterns: How to incorporate design patterns into your mobile app. https://developer.apple.com/library/ios/#referencelibrary/GettingStarted/RoadMapiOS/chapters/Streamline

YourAppswithDesignPatterns/StreamlineYourApps/StreamlineYourApps
.html

- Design Your App With Care: Tips on how best to turn your idea into an app that will be appealing to users. https://developer.apple.com/library/ios/referencelibrary/GettingStarted/RoadMapiOS/chapters/DesignYourAppwithCare/DesignYourAppWithCare/DesignYourAppWithCare.html

- Know the Core Objects of Your App: This is a review of the UIKit objects included in the app and the role each plays. https://developer.apple.com/library/ios/#referencelibrary/GettingStarted/RoadMapiOS/chapters/KnowtheCoreObjectsofYourApp/KnowCoreAppObjects/KnowCoreApp Objects.html

- Internationalize Your App: Teaches you how to make your app available in multiple languages. https://developer.apple.com/library/ios/referencelibrary/GettingStarted/RoadMapiOS/chapters/InternationalizeYourApp/InternationalizeYourApp/InternationalizeYourApp.html

Android Programming Tutorials

These online tutorials offer programmers a guide to ensuring that their Android app turns out the way they wanted. Tutorials include basics on getting started, user experience, and security concerns.

- Getting Started: Tips on building your first app, managing the activity life cycle, supporting different devices, building a dynamic UI with fragments, saving data, interacting with other apps, and sharing content. http://developer.android.com/training/index.html

- Building Apps with Multimedia: Tips on managing audio playback and capturing photos. http://developer.android.com/training/building-multimedia.html

- Building Apps with Graphics & Animation: Tips on displaying bitmaps efficiently, displaying graphics with OpenGL ES, and adding animations. http://developer.android.com/training/building-graphics.html

- Building Apps with Connectivity & the Cloud: Tips on connecting devices wirelessly, performing network operations, transferring data without draining the battery, and syncing to the Cloud. http://developer.android.com/training/building-connectivity.html

■ Building Apps with User Info & Location: Tips on accessing contacts data, remembering users, and making your app location aware. http://developer.android.com/training/building-userinfo.html

■ Best Practices for User Experience & UI: Tips on designing effective navigation, implementing effective navigation, notifying the user, adding search functionality, designing for multiple screens, designing for TV, creating custom views, creating backward-compatible UIs, and implementing accessibility. http://developer.android.com/training/best-ux.html

■ Best Practices for User Input: Tips on using touch gestures and handling keyboard input. http://developer.android.com/training/best-user-input.html

■ Best Practices for Performance: Tips for improving layout performance, running in a background service, loading data in the background, optimizing battery life, sending operations to multiple threads, and keeping your app responsive. http://developer.android.com/training/best-performance.html

■ Best Practices for Security & Privacy: Tips on security with HTTPS and SSL and developing for enterprise. http://developer.android.com/training/best-security.html

DIY Services

These online services give developers with no programming experience the opportunity to quickly and easily build a functioning app:

■ ANZ Hosting: www.anzhosting.com

■ AppBreeder: www.appbreeder.com

■ appsbar: www.appsbar.com

■ AppsBuilder: www.apps-builder.com/en/home

■ Build an App: www.buildanapp.com

■ iBuild App: http://ibuildapp.com

- Make Me Droid: www.makemedroid.com/en

- Mippin: http://mippin.com

- Mobincube: www.mobincube.com

- The AppBuilder: www.theappbuilder.com

Hiring Freelance Programmers

These online sites offer developers without programming experience the ability to link up with programmers and coders who have the skills needed to build their mobile app:

- AppBooker: www.appbooker.com

- Elance: www.elance.com/r/contractors/q-Mobile/cat-it-programming/ind-true

- Freelancer: www.freelancer.com/work/freelance-mobile-app-developer

- Freelancers Outpost: www.freelancersoutpost.com/freelance-mobile-app-development-jobs

- GetAppQuotes: www.getappquotes.com

- Girapps: http://girapps.com/

- Mobileappfreelance: http://mobileappfreelance.com

- NewAppIdea: www.newappidea.com

Hiring a Digital Agency

Developers willing to invest more money in building their mobile app will most likely look for a digital agency, which provides a team of specialists to code and program an app. These sites provide developers with contact information for and background on various digital agencies across the country:

- Agency Spotter: www.agencyspotter.com

- Award Winning Agencies Database: www.awardwinninginteractiveagencies.com

- Best Web Design Agencies: www.bestwebdesignagencies.com
- Fab Hire: www.fabhire.com
- SourcingLine: www.sourcingline.com
- Top Interactive Agencies: www.topinteractiveagencies.com

Testing Services

These sites offer developers the opportunity to test out their mobile app before sending it to the app stores to make sure it is bug-free.

- Elusive Stars: www.elusivestars.com
- iBetaTest: http://ibetatest.com
- TestFlight: www.testflight.com
- The Beta Family: http://thebetafamily.com
- UserTesting: www.usertesting.com

Appeal Help

If your app ends up getting rejected by the app stores, these online sites will walk you through the process of appealing the decision.

- Apple: https://developer.apple.com/appstore/contact/?topic=appeal
- Google Play: https://support.google.com/googleplay/android-developer/contact/appappeals

In-App Advertising Services

One way to make money off your app is to include in-app advertising. These are the online services that match up app developers with advertisers:

- AdMob: www.google.com.my/ads/admob
- iAd: http://advertising.apple.com
- Leadbolt: www.leadbolt.com

- mMedia: http://mmedia.com

- MobFox: www.mobfox.com

- mobhero: www.mobhero.com

- Mojiva: www.mojiva.com

- SendDroid: http://senddroid.com

- Tapjoy: www.tapjoy.com

- ValueClick Media: www.valueclickmedia.com

Price Drop Sites

These sites provide consumers with a constantly updated look at which apps are being lowered in price. Getting highlighted by one of these sites is a great way to draw consumers to your app.

- AppShopper: http://appshopper.com

- ioSnoops: www.iosnoops.com/iphone-ipad-apps-on-sale

App and Website Domain Name Generators

These sites help to devise names for both mobile apps and web domains for developers having trouble coming up with something catchy and creative.

- DomainGroovy: http://domaingroovy.com/website-name-generator

- Dot-o-mator: www.dotomator.com

- NameBoy: http://nameboy.com

- NameFind: www.namefind.com

- Panabee: www.panabee.com

App Icon Generators

Developers without money for a graphic designer can turn to these online sites to help design and create a memorable icon.

- Easy App Icon Maker: http://graphicriver.net/item/easy-app-icon-maker/2563742

- Icon Slayer: www.gieson.com/Library/projects/utilities/icon_slayer/#.Uc4e6eukCeo

- img2icns: www.img2icnsapp.com

- iOS 7 App Icon Kit: http://medialoot.com/item/iphone-app-icon-kit

- MakeAppIcon: http://makeappicon.com

Registering and Building a Website

These sites will help developers register domain names for company and app websites and provide all the tools to actually build them.

- Bluehost: www.bluehost.com

- Domain.com: www.domain.com

- FatCow: www.fatcow.com

- GoDaddy: www.godaddy.com

- iPage: www.ipage.com

- Just Host: www.justhost.com

- Network Solutions: www.networksolutions.com

- 1&1: www.1and1.com

- Register.com: www.register.com

- Web.com: www.web.com

Mobile App-Review Sites

These online sites review mobile apps for consumers. They are a good place to turn to when trying to increase publicity around your app.

- AppAddict.net: http://appaddict.net
- The Appera: http://theappera.com
- AppFreak: http://AppFreakBlog.com
- AppGamer.net: http://appgamer.net
- The AppGoddess.com: www.theappgoddess.com
- AppModo: http://appmodo.com
- Appotography: http://Appotography.com
- Apps and Hats: http://appsandhats.com
- appSIZED: www.appsized.com
- AppSmile: www.appsmile.com
- AppStruck: http://appstruck.com
- The Canadian Reviewer: www.canadianreviewer.com
- Gamezbo: www.gamezebo.com
- iGame Radio: www.igameradio.com
- Insanely Great Mac: www.insanely-great.com
- iPad Insight: www.ipadinsight.com
- iPhoneCaptain: http://iPhoneCaptain.com
- iPhone Gamer Blog: www.iphonegamerblog.com
- iPhone Life magazine: http://iphonelife.com
- iPhone Reviews 2.0: http://ifonereviews.blogspot.com
- iSource: http://iSource.com
- iTito Themes Blog: http://ititothemes.wordpress.com
- iTracki: www.itracki.com

- Life in LoFi: iPhoneography: http://lifeinlofi.com
- Macworld Appguide: www.macworld.com/category/ios-apps
- No DPad: http://nodpad.com
- 148Apps: http://148Apps.com
- OneClickMac: www.oneclickmac.com
- The Portable Gamer: http://theportablegamer.com
- Razorianfly: www.razorianfly.com
- SlapApp.com: http://slapapp.com
- Slide to Play: http://slidetoplay.com
- Today in iOS: http://tii.libsyn.com
- TouchMyApps: http://touchmyapps.com
- TouchGen: http://touchgen.com

Index

About the Author

Chad Brooks has logged nearly fifteen years in the media business. He started his career at the *Daily Herald* in suburban Chicago, where he spent more than a decade covering an array of topics, including local and state government, crime and the legal system, and education. Following his years at the newspaper, Brooks transitioned to public relations, where he helped to promote small businesses across the country, landing media placements for his clients in local, regional, and national outlets. During that time, he gained a unique perspective on what it takes to launch and sustain a successful small business. Today, Brooks spends his time as a Chicago-based freelance writer, covering business and technology stories for a number of online outlets. His work regularly appears in BusinessNewsDaily, the Huffington Post, Yahoo!, and Fox Business.